PENGUIN BOOKS

TEACHING THINKING

Edward de Bono was born in Malta and after his initial education at St Edward's College, Malta, and the Royal University of Malta, where he obtained a degree in medicine, he proceeded as a Rhodes Scholar to Christ Church, Oxford, where he gained an honours degree in psychology and physiology and then a D.Phil. in medicine. He also holds a Ph.D. from Cambridge. He has had faculty appointments at the universities of Oxford, London, Cambridge and Harvard.

Dr de Bono runs the largest curriculum programme for the direct teaching of thinking in schools. Some countries, like Venezuela, have made it compulsory in all schools, and there is a growing use in Canada, the USA, China and Russia. Dr de Bono's instruction in thinking has also been sought by such well-known corporations as NTT (Japan), Du Pont, Ericsson, United Technologies, American Standard, Exxon and Shell. His 'Six Hats' method is now used in many corporations, such as Prudential and IBM. He has also worked for governments, including the Government of California on toxic waste problems. He may be teaching senior executives of multinational corporations one day and nine-year-olds in a primary school the next.

Dr de Bono has been invited to address such meetings as The Institute of Institutional Investors, The Commonwealth Law Conference, The American Bar Association, The World Congress on Emergency and Disaster Medicine, The World Economic Forum (Davos) and The Society of Information Managers. In 1989 he chaired a meeting of Nobel Prize laureates in Seoul, Korea.

He is the founder and director of the Cognitive Research Trust (1969). He has also founded the International Creative Forum which has as members the leading corporations world-wide in each field (Du Pont, Merck, British Airways, etc.). He has set up an International Creativity Office to help the UN develop fresh alternatives as required.

Dr de Bono has been invited to lecture and work in forty-five countries. He has written over thirty-six books and there are translations available in twenty-six languages, including Chinese, Korean, Japanese,

Russian, Arabic, Hebrew, Urdu, Bahasa and all major languages. He has made two television series, 'De Bono's Course in Thinking' for the BBC and 'The Greatest Thinkers' for WDR, Germany. He runs a newsletter which is published ten times a year and is the inventor of the classic L-Game which is said to be the simplest real game ever invented. He is perhaps best known for originating the term 'lateral thinking', which now has an entry in the Oxford English Dictionary. The organiser of the very successful 1984 Olympic Games attributed their success to the use of lateral thinking, which he had first learned from Dr de Bono in 1975.

Other titles published by Penguin:

Atlas of Management Thinking
Children Solve Problems
Conflicts: A Better Way to Resolve Them
Edward de Bono's Masterthinker's Handbook
The Five-Day Course in Thinking
Future Positive
Handbook for the Positive Revolution
The Happiness Purpose
I Am Right You Are Wrong
Lateral Thinking
Lateral Thinking for Management
Letters to Thinkers
The Mechanism of Mind
Opportunities
Po: Beyond Yes and No
Practical Thinking
Six Thinking Hats
The Use of Lateral Thinking
Wordpower

Dr Edward de Bono is world-renowned for his work in the area of creative thinking. His international seminars are invariably a sell-out. For further information please contact The McQuaig Group, 132 Rochester Ave., Toronto M4N 1P1, Canada. Tel: (416) 488-0008.

Edward de Bono

Teaching Thinking

Penguin Books

PENGUIN BOOKS

Published by the Penguin Group
Penguin Books Ltd, 27 Wrights Lane, London W8 5TZ, England
Penguin Books USA Inc., 375 Hudson Street, New York, New York 10014, USA
Penguin Books Australia Ltd, Ringwood, Victoria, Australia
Penguin Books Canada Ltd, 10 Alcorn Avenue, Toronto, Ontario, Canada M4V 3B2
Penguin Books (NZ) Ltd, 182–190 Wairau Road, Auckland 10, New Zealand

Penguin Books Ltd, Registered Offices: Harmondsworth, Middlesex, England

First published by Maurice Temple Smith Ltd 1976
Published in Pelican Books 1978
Reprinted in Penguin Books 1991
10 9 8 7 6 5 4 3 2

Printed in England by Clays Ltd, St Ives plc
Set in Linotype Juliana

Contents

Foreword

I should like this to be a gentle book that makes a few definite and practical points, upsets no one and gives help and encouragement to those who have always felt that thinking could be taught directly as a skill. But the book will not, I fear, be taken as such. It will be seen to be arrogant and dogmatic. It will be seen to ignore the work of everyone else. It will be seen unnecessarily to attack cows that have earned their right to be sacred. Although I can foresee all this I cannot avoid it without diluting the purpose of the book.

The book is not a treatise on thinking or on teaching. My main aim is to avoid confusion. For that reason the easements and qualifications that could have surrounded many points have been left out, with the result that the point must seem arrogant and dogmatic. The subject of thinking is surrounded by misconceptions and concepts fossilized by increments of hallowed tradition. To free some of the concepts it may sometimes be necessary to chip away with harsh force. Yet the intention is mild. For instance I may appear to attack logic, that mainstay of our thinking culture. And yet I shall not be attacking logic at all. I shall be attacking the *exclusivity* of logic, in order to bring forward the importance of the perception stage of thinking. I stand with everyone else in my acknowledgement of the vital importance of logic for the *processing stage of thinking*. I am aware that a lot of people have done good work in this field of 'thinking'. Nevertheless this book is not consciously derived from their work although I am sure there must be much parallelism and overlap. Nor is it intended as a passive library review of work in the field.

The book is intended to deal in a practical and personal manner with the teaching of thinking. It is not philosophical speculation, but is based on what may well be the largest programme anywhere in the world for the direct teaching of thinking as a skill and, quite apart from this, on considerable experience in the teaching of thinking to somewhat demanding pupils. Above all I should like the book to be of use to teachers who want to teach thinking directly as a skill. We know from experience that the needs of the teacher who is actually going to do something are very different from the needs of a teacher who is just going to talk about doing something. The former is practical and wishes not to be confused. The latter prefers the subject to be handled with enough subtlety and comparison and enrichment to provide talking-points.

Thinking is a most awkward subject to handle. It always involves resentment. It is felt that you are suggesting that the thinking of other people is not as good as it might be – or, worse, that your own thinking is better. Let me declare firmly at this stage that the motor mechanic is not the *grand prix* driver. Tinkering and fiddling with thinking on the design side are not the same as being an ace performer. The difficulty is that thinking is so closely involved with the ego that in all except young children *thinking is the ego*. Criticize someone's thinking or suggest an inadequacy and you threaten that person's ego in the same manner. Very few people can so detach themselves that they can look at their own thinking on some matter and describe it as feeble.

Much of the awkwardness arises from the word 'thinking'. This is such an ordinary word that it is as much part of life as seeing, hearing, talking, walking and breathing. And no one feels he needs to be taught how to do any of these things. We could call it 'cognitive studies' (or cognetics, as one class called it), but that would be jargon and pompous. Exactly the same problem arose with 'creativity' and 'lateral thinking'. Creativity is a value word and represents a value judgement – no one ever calls creative something new which he dislikes. Creativity also has too many artistic connotations to describe the process of changing concepts and perceptions. Many artists have valuable concepts and perceptions but are not specially good at changing them. So it was necessary to create the neutral label 'lateral thinking' to describe the change from one way of looking at things to another. We need to do the same with 'thinking' in order to separate what goes on in our heads all the time from the more focused thinking that has a purpose. But a new label would sound too artificial and would cause too much resentment. In specific cases the problem usually solves itself. For instance users of the Cognitive Research Trust programme for teaching thinking just refer to it as CoRT Thinking, or even Cort.

As will become apparent in this book, we also need a much better word than 'perception' for the-way-we-look-at-things. Perception is too abstract, too psychological and too concerned with visual and other sensory perception to cope with the way the *mind* looks at things. One day I may find the right word for this, but I do not have one yet.

A new label for 'thinking' might also avoid the centipede problem. Many people are frightened that if they become too self-conscious about their thinking processes they will, like the centipede, lie distracted in the ditch wondering how to perform all that happened naturally before they were made self-conscious about it.

In spite of the awkwardness of the subject I have enjoyed teaching thinking in a variety of classrooms. The range extends from a class of nine-year-olds in Australia to a group of men each of whom handled over one billion dollars a year, and who together managed what must be the largest block of capital in the western world. Of course it has been possible to teach thinking only because the pupils have been interested in the subject. The interest has been surprising. In Britain alone I have been asked to speak at eighty per cent of all universities, often to departments as widely separated as metallurgy and psychology. Thinking knows no boundaries. Interest has been shown by artists, architects, surveyors, computer analysts, advertisers, system designers, operations-research scientists, business executives, investment managers, bankers, personnel managers, teachers, principals, educationalists, mathematicians, physicists, chemists, engineers, journalists, lawyers, librarians, prison officers, fire departments, government departments and so on. The only unifying factor is that these people have been 'doers', not 'describers'. They are people who have to use their thinking to bring something about. They are people who have felt a need for generative thinking in addition to the critical thinking with which education had endowed them.

In all I suppose I must have taught thinking directly to about 120,000 people face to face (excluding books and other media) and the most surprising thing is the uniformity of reaction at a basic thinking level across wide ranges of age, ability and interest. From Argentina to Sweden, from Australia to Switzerland, from Japan to Canada the fundamental human thinking operations seem very similar, even though the overlying temperament and behaviour may be different. Perhaps this is not so surprising.

What has surprised me is the huge interest in the idea of treating thinking as a skill that can be improved by attention. I had been led to believe by various sages in the education field that teachers and heads would resent any attempt to treat thinking as a skill, on the grounds that that is what schools were already doing all the time. On the contrary, there has been a very positive response, based on a feeling that thinking skill was not quite the same as accumulation of knowledge or innate intelligence.

The book is divided into two parts. The first part deals with the general principles involved in the teaching of thinking. I attempt to show the need for teaching thinking as a skill, and a conceptual framework is also provided. The comments and ideas in this section are based on my observations both on thinking as a phenomenon and also on the teaching of thinking. Many of the points that I shall be making are not at all new, sensational or exotic. It would be absurd to pretend that only newness had value. Some of the observations may be new, some of the conclusions or concepts may be new, but others will already be part of the thinking of many readers. I see no reason for eschewing those aspects upon which most people are agreed. I hope that the book will serve to reinforce and re-emphasize those well-accepted ideas and show how they contribute to the teaching of thinking as a skill. The aim of the book is to be practical rather than exotic.

The second part of the book is based directly on practical experience. Many books of this nature tend to become interesting discussions on the possibility of teaching thinking as a skill, or reviews of a variety of small-scale attempts at such teaching. The second part of this one is firmly based on the experience acquired from the wide use of a particular programme. Much of that experience relates to the general problems that arise when thinking is treated as a skill. Some of it relates specifically to the particular nature of the programme used. Some of it relates to what happens when any innovation is introduced into the school curriculum. The programme is a continuing one, so a final analysis of the project is not available. Nevertheless sufficient experience has accumulated to be of value to those who are interested in teaching thinking as a skill. Inevitably it will seem that references to the programme are intended to sell the virtues of this particular programme. I see no way of avoiding this except by these protestations here. It is not possible to talk about something and yet not talk about it. I must leave it to readers to read the comments objectively and to extract general principles. Above all I wanted to avoid the sort of book which might intrigue the reader, only for him or her to say at the end: 'That's all very interesting in theory, but what happens when you are trying to teach thinking to a class of thirty children facing you on a Monday morning?' The comments in the second part of the book are based on that sort of situation.

Finally I should like to urge the reader to take from the book whatever constructive ideas he may find rather than regarding it as a source of philosophical points with which he can enjoy disagreeing.

EDWARD DE BONO
Cambridge 1975

Introduction

'A schoolgirl wants to train to be a teacher. Her father has to live abroad for five years because of his work, and her mother is going with him. Should the girl go with them or stay with relatives or friends so that she can finish school and do the training?' This problem was given to some children (ten- and eleven-year-olds) at a school which contained many army children, so the problem was relevant to their own lives. Eight separate groups of children discussed the problem and the discussions were tape-recorded. The groups who had not had any training in thinking considered the following numbers of aspects of the problem: 3, 5, 5, 5. The groups who had had ten thinking lessons considered rather more aspects: 17, 17, 19, 13 (see results section for fuller details). Being taught thinking directly as a skill can therefore make a difference.

We assume that education teaches thinking. This is correct. Manifestly schools do not teach un-thinking. We are complacent. As one teacher said at a meeting: 'We don't need to learn to think. We're all right, aren't we?' Our best pupils pass the exams which education has set up as a test of their ability. Our most brilliant pupils come out of our best universities as brilliant graduates. But we must not forget that it is a self-fulfilling system. Education sets up its own exams to test how well it is preparing pupils for those exams. Nor must we forget the 'archway effect' which states that if a stream of brilliant people go towards an archway, then from that archway will emerge a stream of brilliant people, even if the archway has done no more than straddle their passage. Perhaps our élite universities do not produce brilliant graduates because of the excellence of their teaching, but because they take only brilliant undergraduates. Does education really teach thinking skills?

Mathematics is a highly effective thinking system made even more effective by our invention of the computer. Thanks to mathematics we can perform such unthinkable feats as landing men on the moon, letting them drive round on the surface, hearing and watching them do it, and then bringing them safely back to earth. We can harness atomic energy itself. Where we can use mathematics it is a superb thinking system. But getting to the moon is easier than solving urban poverty, juvenile delinquency or even a simple strike. In space things remain constant. We can translate the situation into definite symbols and relationships and then deal fluently with these. On the surface of the earth, however, most situations are vague, interrelated, subjectively defined, shifting in value and dependent on human whims. Very, very rarely do we have even half the information we need to solve the problem – and yet we have to take action. If only we could translate all situations into definite symbols and relationships we should never need to look beyond mathematics for our thinking. One day we may be able to, but that day is a long way off because any problem involving human perception and values will always contain a lot of unknowns and unknowables. Sadly the world is not at all like those school mathematics problems in which all the information you need is given and all you have to do is to apply the right process and extract the result. Alas!

God does not need to think: thinking is used only to supplement inadequate knowledge. Too often there is a god-like attitude in education. If only we could increase knowledge then we would throw out doubt, indecision and problems. We pile on the knowledge. Knowledge is easy to teach and knowledge is there. Indeed knowledge is growing at such a rapid rate that there is little time to teach anything else. Statistics have almost wrecked science because statistics seem to generate knowledge. It is felt (quite wrongly) that if you generate enough data an idea will emerge. So funds are poured into data-mongering, with never a thought for the ideas that used to provoke science in the old days. Education teaches knowledge because there is nothing else to teach. But knowledge is no more a substitute for thinking than thinking is a substitute for knowledge. In most of the practical situations of life knowledge is never going to be complete (if only because so many situations deal with the future), so thinking is going to be needed. Perhaps we teach a knowledge subject on the assumption that thinking skills will be developed in the course of our having to deal with the knowledge. If thinking skills are our objective then the by-product approach is not a very effective method, since knowledge has its own internal momentum which makes it difficult to pay attention to, or develop, thinking skills. There are too many brilliant academics whose brilliance in their own fields and lack of it outside those fields shows the difference between knowledge and thinking.

We often mistake fluency and argumentation for thinking skill. Fluency and the power of coherent expression are tools of thinking, not thinking itself. Error-free thinking is not necessarily good thinking, as will be discussed in detail later. Very able pupils usually react to an idea by making an initial judgement ('I like it', 'It will never work' and so on). They then use reason and skilled argument to back up that initial judgement. The argument may be flawless, yet the thinking may be appalling because it includes those major perceptual errors of looking at only part of the situation or ignoring the magnitude of effects. We also confuse debating skills with thinking: 'I can prove you wrong, *therefore* I am right.'

We come now to the major deficiency in our traditional approach to thinking. Above all education prides itself on its success in training the *critical intelligence*. In fact this is often put forward, in print and in speech, as the supreme aim of education. Why? Is lack of error enough? If we can find faults in systems and ideas we may escape the tragedy of being dominated by them – but does that enable us to construct more usable systems? There are three reasons for our adoration of the critical intelligence. First, criticism is easy, possibly the easiest form of intellectual achievement, and it is a joy to operate since there is something definite to get to work upon and some definite result. Secondly, critical thinking allows us to work in the comfortable self-contained environment of the available data without having to worry about getting fresh data: we look for internal validity, internal consistency. Thirdly, education was for a long time in the hands

of the ecclesiastical authorities who founded most of our élite educational establishments and so established the traditions of education. Critical thinking is of paramount importance in the
ecclesiastical world since it is the only weapon against heresy and
deviation and since that world consists of concept edifices which
must have internal validity if they are not to collapse. But all that
is very far from the practical, messy world in which people have to
think (with very inadequate data) in order to solve problems and
bring things about. Critical intelligence is very valuable. Critical
thinking is an essential part of thinking. But it can never be the
whole of thinking.

In education we rightly put great emphasis on understanding
and analysis. We rightly extol scholarship because scholarship is
valuable and because scholars are what the system prides itself on
producing. But passive, descriptive, contemplative thinking – no
matter how subtle or acute – is not the same as generative thinking. Generative thinking is concerned with bringing things about
and solving problems. Generative thinking is practical, creative
and constructive. Generative thinking has to deal with the
world and take action, even if knowledge is incomplete. Generative thinking cannot ask the world to wait while it applies itself
in scholarly fashion to generating that sufficiency of knowledge
on which action can properly be based. Active thinking (generative) and passive thinking (scholarly) are not mutually exclusive.
We need both. But education must free itself from the impractical
myth that scholarly excellence will solve everything. Critical
thinking, scholarly thinking and generative thinking all have
their place. I don't mind in what order of importance they are
placed. I am only concerned that education should take notice of
generative thinking. Generative thinking is messy, imperfect,
impure and perhaps difficult to teach. But it is important and we
should try to teach it.

Teaching thinking

Teaching thinking is as difficult as walking a tightrope. That is to
say, it is easy if you do not fall off. Thinking is intangible. It is

awkward. It gets into so many places that it is never in any one place. Yet over the years we have built up certain concepts of what thinking is all about. The difficulty lies in keeping one's balance and avoiding falling into, and being trapped by, these concepts.

'You want to teach thinking. Ah yes, that is logic. You know, we have always taught logic.'

'We have always encouraged them to think. Yesterday we were having a discussion on famine in Ethiopia and they were really thinking hard about what could be done to help.'

On the one hand it is easy to find oneself teaching logic, the rules of logic, computer logic and perhaps even mathematical logic. On the other hand it is possible to find oneself having long, and interesting, discussions about some topic in the belief that talking about something is the same as teaching thinking skills. It is also possible to find oneself looking at thinking in an objective manner: analysing the process into philosophical or psychological concepts. One might find oneself agreeing with the teacher who claimed: 'You cannot teach thinking. You can only teach things to think about.' One may also dispute any distinction between intelligence and thinking skill and suppose that thinking is nothing more than the visible operation of innate intelligence.

There are all sorts of preconceptions and misconceptions that surround the subject of thinking, and especially the teaching of thinking. This book is about a particular approach to the subject of thinking itself, and a practical approach to the teaching of thinking. It is best not to have any preconceptions and to let the intangible subject of thinking gel into something definite and usable in the course of the book. The most difficult audiences in the world are not sceptical, reluctant ones but the eager ones who rush off into paths of misconstruction so readily that the speaker spends all his time trying to pull them back. There is nothing worse than a person who says, 'Yes, I know about that' when he does not; or 'Yes, I do that' when he does not. Negation or opposition are very much easier to deal with than apparent agreement. Any school that believes it is already doing all there is to be done about teaching thinking is far less likely to be doing anything than a school which derides the idea of treating thinking as a skill.

Thinking and society

There was a time when society was comparatively stable and, since things did not change much, repetition was a good substitute for thinking. The political systems tended to be élitist and a few people did the thinking for the rest. To make personal decisions and problem-solving easier there were the guidelines laid down by religious doctrine and moral codes. Much as we may like to revert to the good aspects of those more stable times, we must acknowledge that society is no longer so stable because the rate of change, fuelled by technology and social aspirations, has accelerated. In such a complex society the need for thinking is greater than ever. We have more freedom and freedom represents a tyranny of opportunity, since each opportunity is a potential decision. Yet the powerful substitutes for thinking (habit, doctrine, dogma, someone else doing the thinking) have been much weakened. In their place there has emerged only one aid to thinking – 'thinking by slogan'. A slogan is not part of a general system of attitudes, but just an encapsulated attitude to a particular circumstance that has not emerged because of its intrinsic merit or even its general acceptability, but because it has those characteristics which suit the media. Just as an attractive television personality is more use to a politician than economic understanding, so a media-powerful slogan is more effective than a wise one. It is not the fault of the media or of anyone else – it is simply due to the structure of the system.

On a personal level, people have to do more thinking and make more decisions than ever before. There are more opportunities and more pressures. There is more social mobility, there are more career opportunities; there is more money to be spent; divorce is easier and emotional expectations are higher; authoritarian control systems are weaker and so much that used to be ordered in society or taken for granted has now become a matter for individual thinking.

On a political level many countries enjoy or seem to enjoy a democratic system. It doesn't really matter whether the party machines allow those elected to be truly representative of the electorate. What does matter is that, once they are in power, the politicians do have to pay heed to the opinions, attitudes and preferences of the electorate in order to keep themselves in power. It should be the individual thinking of the electors that determines their attitudes. If they do no thinking then habit or party line or instant television persuasion are the only available substitutes. At either extreme of the political spectrum we have élitism in which a self-designated élite class determines the thinking of the rest, who cannot be trusted to think for themselves. A left-wing teacher once said that he did not approve of a programme to teach everyone to think because in a 'diversified' society some people were going to do the thinking and the rest would follow. There is some point in this. Some people will undoubtedly do more thinking than others (provided it is thinking and not just party doctrine), but it is desirable that the rest should at least do enough thinking to decide for themselves whether the special thinkers make sense or not.

In a complex society political decisions and pressures depend very much on individual thinking. If that thinking can see only narrow self-interest, or only an immediate future, then society becomes a power struggle for self-interest. To some extent it always has been so and perhaps it is only the location of power that has changed. Nevertheless society is much more complex than it has ever been and perhaps the old power games are no longer the best way to run things. For instance it requires quite a lot of individual thinking to change from the concept of growth and greed to one of restraint and stability.

It may seem, and it is often argued, that thinking makes matters more complex and that gut reaction is a more direct prelude to action. This attitude arises from the notion that thinking is about 'puzzling things out' rather than 'seeing things more clearly'. Far from confusing matters thinking should serve to simplify them. To make a decision when you can see only one course of action is easier than having to choose between two possible courses, but is such blindness really helpful? To remove the fear of thinking we need to make it very matter-of-fact and routine. That is exactly what teaching thinking is all about.

There are a few people who believe that teaching thinking is dangerous, much as 'a little learning is a dangerous thing.' It is felt that if people start thinking for themselves they may ask awkward questions and refuse to take for granted those things which need to be taken for granted. But sooner or later people are going to start thinking for themselves. There is no way of stopping them, except with a powerful party line which pre-empts this activity. It may be better to learn to think in an open fashion rather than let thinking be only an expression of emotional discontent. On a recent visit to Australia I was asked by someone concerned with a social studies programme why it was assumed that children would be against something as soon as they started to think about it. In his experience, and in mine, the opposite seemed to be the case: when children did think about some aspect of society they often came to appreciate why things had to be done in a certain way. For instance when children think about school rules they often suggest even tougher rules.

A headmaster once told me that it was *unfair* to teach people how to think. He said that most of the pupils from his school were going to spend their lives at factory benches and that thinking would only make them dissatisfied. I can see his point but I do not agree. If he really believed what he said then education would set out to create zombies perfectly fitted to the task society demanded of them. Quite apart from the likelihood that electronic robots will continue to take over more and more of the routine factory tasks, there is no conflict between simple tasks and thinking. In the days of the monasteries the most abstruse and élite theological thinkers used to spend their days in everyday farming or gardening or craftwork. To be sure these activities were more pleasant than factory tasks, but they were just as routine. It has even been argued that a routine task (like Churchill's famous bricklaying) actually frees the mind to do some thinking. This is a poor excuse for keeping jobs boring, but it does indicate that the level of mechanical activity need not limit the level of mental activity. I think few people would accept the deliberate anaesthetizing or zombification of people as one of the tasks of education.

Thinking should not be a replacement for gut feeling, religious belief, political identity or commitment. All these have their place and their value in the rich fabric of humanity. Emotion is what matters in the end, since it is the final arbiter of human value. But true emotion can just as easily follow clear perception as precede it. Emotion that precedes perception leads to prejudice and the tyranny of temperament.

Many people argue that thinking can never be neutral, that it must always be moral or political and that to teach thinking is to teach some particular political idiom. It is true that to decide to teach thinking is a political decision, since some political systems would prefer people to follow rather than think. But beyond that teaching thinking is neutral. Using a microscope is not of itself a political activity. A microscope is a device to enlarge our vision. Thinking is a device to enlarge our perception. Thinking is as neutral as a pair of spectacles. To deny someone spectacles because with clearer vision they might find you out is a political decision. It is just as possible that with the spectacles they would see a wider context and come to understand and appreciate what is being done. It is only deception that fears clear vision.

Teaching thinking and the curriculum

There are times when teachers, principals, educationalists and politicians find it necessary to put down the aims and objectives of education. Invariably, the list of objectives is headed by 'teaching pupils to think for themselves'. It seems obvious that this must be the underlying aim of education and that all else stems from this. Unfortunately the universality of the lip service (or pen service) paid to this aim is not matched by any practical attempt to teach thinking as a skill. In all fairness it must be said that no one *dares* admit that the by-product method of teaching thinking as a spin-off from the teaching of all other subjects is ineffective. To admit this would impose upon the education system a huge burden of effort and change.

Above all education has to be a practical system. The survival of such a huge and complex system depends on a tight, interlocking structure and a lot of necessary inertia. Most of the subjects taught in the curriculum are there because they were there yesterday. It would be a hard task to justify the necessity for any single subject apart from language and mathematics. On the other hand it would be an impossible task to show that any subject was useless. For every traditional subject there are teachers used to teaching that subject, ways of teaching it, textbooks and work sheets, examinations and timetable slots. Since children do turn up at school and do have to be taught, it is easier to carry through those subjects for which established teachers and teaching methods exist. So it should be. Physics is taught in the curriculum because at one time physics embraced the whole of science. This is no longer the case, but physics is there and it is interesting so it continues to be taught. In fact there is a far greater need in society for chemists and engineers than for physicists (a ratio of at least a hundred to one), yet far fewer pupils have an opportunity to do these subjects. If we look at administration, finance, business studies we find a hugely important area that is virtually neglected at school level because it does not seem to have the teachable purity of physics. I once asked a roomful of about 150 physics students at a university how many of them wanted a career in physics. Less than one in five wanted such a career. The rest intended to go into business or administration. But at school they had done physics and liked it, because no other subjects offered constructive thinking. Because they had done well in their exams in physics they had chosen to do it at university. And so on.

At one meeting a teacher commented: 'Only five per cent of those doing A-level geography will use geography skills in their lives.' The usual argument is that pupils need a broad education including most of the traditional subjects. More specifically, it is felt that teaching any subject trains the mind, as was once said of Latin – for lack of any better justification. These are not honest arguments. The true, and most valid, argument is that something has to be taught and these subjects are there to teach. What else would a teacher be teaching? To be sure, schools are bombarded with suggested new subjects such as social studies, environmental studies, CoRT Thinking and so on. But there is no way of proving that they are effective or useful until after they have been used. There are no teachers experienced in using them. The material is costly and makes obsolete the investment in material for the displaced subject. The timetable is crowded and the new subject cannot be fitted in without displacing another subject. Finally, no examinations have been set up in the subject. It is easy to forget what a stranglehold school-leaving or university-entrance examinations exert on the curriculum. The exams are there and they are competitive. So schools have an obligation to train their pupils to succeed in these exams. The exams test the traditional subjects. The traditional subjects have to be taught because the exams are in these subjects. The system is thus locked in. An individual principal or teacher might wish to teach other subjects but he feels that his responsibility is towards his pupils and that he must give them a chance to get to university. He is sure that that is what the parents would want. So he must put his personal feelings on one side and follow the system as it exists.

The tragedy of the pyramid system in education is that we teach the broad base of the pyramid as if each member were going to reach the peak. We teach for the peak, not for the base or some middle point. We do not say: 'We need so much mathematics but no more'. If the mathematics is there and the pupils are able we just go on teaching it to levels which are quite unrelated to general use. It would be inconceivable for a teacher to stop teaching mathematics when the material is there, the pupils are able, there is time and the examination is there. We teach towards the Einsteins and forget about the shopkeepers. Mediocrity is unscholarly and unacademic, even though a small increase in ability across society may be more valuable than a few more people at the peak (who would probably have got there anyway).

At each point in the system each person is acting sensibly, reasonably and even progressively, yet the sum total of these individuals is a system that must go on teaching material that is becoming less and less relevant to the needs of society. Of course people do need to know history, but perhaps they need even more to know how society works.

The Cognitive Research Trust has many hours of tape-recorded discussions from schools and from these it is obvious that very few pupils have any idea of how the productive or administrative functions of society are carried out. But they know about Henry

VIII. History can be taught and there are exams in history, and everyone knows, quite rightly, that a historical perspective is very necessary.

A business can invest in a new product. If the product succeeds in the market-place, then more productive effort is channelled in its direction. Education is different. It has no market-place other than its own judgement and exam systems. It cannot risk investment in a new direction because it would be risking the careers of those with whom it experiments. Given the interlocked nature of the system, it is a wonder that any change takes place at all and amazing that so many teachers and principals have been able to involve themselves in the teaching of thinking as a skill.

In a Utopian curriculum one might have a division into: basic skills, background studies, vocational or special-interest studies. The basic skills would include: language, thinking, mathematics, social skills, social awareness. Language must come first, because with it comes communication and without communication nothing much else matters. Thinking skills come next, because they enable an individual to deal with the world and with knowledge. Next come mathematical skills, because mathematics is such a perfect thinking system and many decisions have to be based on an understanding of numbers. Social skills include dealing with other people as individuals or in groups, and perhaps emotional skills. Social awareness includes a thorough understanding of how society works, including some understanding of government, administration, industry, economics, politics and so on. It is perhaps absurd to grade these skills, since all are important. We already teach language. We already teach mathematics, but more from the interest of the subject than for practical use. We can teach thinking as a skill if we so determine. Social and emotional skills are difficult to teach unless we use environmental learning, drama and so on. Nevertheless we should make the effort instead of hoping that this sort of thing will happen naturally or saying that it is not the business of education. Knowledge of how society works is very easy to teach, provided we set out to do so and resist the temptation to go so deeply into any one aspect that we neglect the rest (for instance spending hours on studying pollution and not having any notion of how a shop works).

The background studies would include many of the traditional subjects (geography, history, literature, science subjects, foreign languages and so on) and would be taught in order to provide a perspective on and understanding of the world to supplement the basic skills for dealing with the world. There would be no attempt to teach these subjects in examination detail or comprehensiveness. The teaching would be made attractive enough for the subjects to generate the sort of interest that wild-life films or period series on television generate.

The third division would include special or vocational interests. Vocational interests could include business studies, engineering, drama, design, foreign languages and so on. Special interest subjects could include detailed study of periods in history or biological phenomena or literature (somewhat like a university Ph.D. area).

This is a Utopian view, but it contains little that is controversial since most educationalists would agree with the generalities and argue only over specific choices of subject or priorities. Many educationalists would feel that some schools are moving towards this system anyway. Alas, this is not true. A few excellent schools get attention and get written about, but compared to the total number of schools their number is infinitesimal. Talking about and doing are different things. A few schools undoubtedly do have an inspired staff and can handle some of the Utopian ideals with ease. Unfortunately this skill is not transferable to other schools unless the inspired staff are transferred as a body. For transfer to other schools and incorporation into the system as a whole there has to be something objective that can be used and a change in structure (for example in exams) which makes it usable. That is why a thinking programme needs a definite structure and form. We could do the same in other areas if we were determined to make the effort and if we contented ourselves with producing something usable rather than something perfect and beyond criticism.

The search for academic perfection is often the enemy of practical education. Anyone who produces material is always conscious of the armchair user, who is going to compare it with the imagined perfection of what could and should be rather than the practical nature of what can be used. Hearing teachers talk on a philosophical level about a teaching programme is very different from listening to teachers who have actually used the lessons.

Teachers often know the practical impossibility of doing something new, and in order to avoid having to face this they erect a dilemma: 'If you give us something simple we shall not be impressed by it because we shall claim we do it anyway. If you give us something complicated we shall be impressed by its seriousness but unable to use it because it is complicated.'

On the whole teachers and principals have been most helpful and encouraging and without their interest the idea of teaching thinking as a skill would have remained an idea. Perhaps the most encouraging response came from a teacher who said that she considered teaching thinking 'almost as essential as reading'.

A headmaster once said of the teaching-thinking programme: 'I don't know what effect it has had on the children but it has certainly made my staff think more.' With sentiments like that about there is not much wrong with the education system that a change in structure and some directed effort cannot put right.

Part One

What is thinking?

There is a difference between the philosophical definition of thinking and thinking in practical use. It is not much use asking children for a philosophical definition of thinking, but they can be asked what they like to think about. I once asked a large number of children to tell me what they like to think about. The replies are divided into the under-twelves and the over-twelves.

Under-twelves

'Princesses, being a teacher, love and marriage.'

'Maths problems and designing clothes.'

'Animals, for example, beetles and dinosaurs.'

'I like thinking about naughty children getting told off and sometimes I like thinking about being kidnapped.'

'Footballers.'

'Problems of time, space and infinity and how things can be improved.'

'I like inventing things like internal-combustion engines and devices for model aeroplanes and brake units and suspension units.'

'I like thinking about how I should improve my personality (I think that in bed).'

'Things that are in my mind at any time: *Colditz* [a television programme], a new school, football, cars, home.'

'I like imagining I'm Tarzan's wife and I'm very strong and brave.'

At this age thinking means a sort of daydreaming, reveries, contemplation, internal story-telling and imagination. It is an *exploration* not of past experience but of projected experience. One or two children talk about problem-solving but most of them like to think about things or situations which are to be enjoyed rather than solved. Some of the children are concerned with themselves, but most of them are concerned with things, objects and situations. With the older age group there is much more egocentricity.

Over-twelves

'Well at school I suppose I like thinking about being brainy. Sometimes I wish I was pretty. And sometimes I wish I wasn't as small as I am.'

'I like thinking about what I am going to do at the weekends and also about our holidays that are coming up. I also like thinking about getting the better of my spiteful needlework teacher.'

'I think about many things. My life, what I shall do tomorrow, what happened today, school, my girl friend.'

'About what sort of life I'd really like to have and what I'll do when I start work.'

'Sports, girls, dirt-clod fights, drama, aeroplanes.'

'Boy friends and boys that I know who I would like to go out with.'

'Pop singers, clothes, pop music.'

'Myself making great social reforms.'

'Sex, and me being a hero such as: As I carry the boat out, over the loudspeaker the commentator says: "And here comes the brilliant oarsman who I am sure will win the race for us" – and all in front of a crowd made up mostly of girls and women.'

'I like thinking about people I know and I like to decide what I feel about fundamental problems and aspects of life such as religion. I also like thinking in long words to enlarge my vocabulary and I like to think of their etymology because I do Latin and it helps me to understand them.'

Again there is an exploration of experience, but this time the self or ego is very much part of that experience. At this point 'thinking' seems to be that which goes on in the mind and is not related to the immediate situation. It is a sort of playing through on the screen of the mind of past or future experience. The purpose seems to be enjoyment or self-indulgence. This is what one might expect from asking the question: 'What do you *like* to think about?'

Definition of thinking

At a lecture, undergraduates, graduates and faculty members of the department of education at a major university were asked to note down their definition of thinking. Very little time was allowed, so the definitions might well have been altered after further consideration.

The first group of definitions simply stated that 'thinking happens':

'Non-material goings-on in the mind.'

'Mental process done by oneself.'

'Generally, any mental process regardless of whether there is a result.'

'The mental processing of data.'

'Process mind goes through when faced with any situation.'

'Thinking: a blend of the metaphysical, chemical, physical and biological.'

Mostly the above definitions state that thinking happens in the mind and that it is a conscious process. The next group of definitions bring in the notion of *purpose*:

'Mental process of rationalizing. Attempt to come to some conclusion about certain things.'

'The process of using one's brain to attempt to solve some problem or to arrive at some conclusion on some particular topic.'

'Creative process concerned with problem-solving.'

'Working something out by the intellectual use of reason.'

'Pursuing an idea to some purpose.'

'Using cognitive faculties to work things out as opposed to being guided by emotions.'

So thinking is a matter of problem-solving or the attempted achievement of some end. Enjoyment, fantasy or self-indulgent daydreaming might also qualify as a purpose.

Purpose of thinking

When a group of teachers of mathematics were asked to define thinking they saw it almost exclusively as a process of *problem-solving.*

'An activity which starts with a problem and aims at solving that problem.'

'Thinking is a process of ordering available information to achieve a solution.'

'The processing of "material" given to solve the various types of problem.'

'Using your ability (intelligence?) to obtain an answer to some problem.'

'Thinking is considering the possibilities which will help you to arrive at a solution to a problem.'

'Thinking is a thought-process to solve problems.'

'Assessment of facts according to one's experience to solve a problem or clarify a situation.'

It is quite possible that 'problem' was used in the general sense of achieving a desired state, in which case any thinking with a desired result can be considered to be 'problem-solving'. But in its narrower sense problem-solving does not include the concept of 'understanding' or 'clarifying a situation'. Too often this process is taken to be part of perception, and thinking is then regarded as the process of working upon the perceptions to solve a problem. In this book thinking will be regarded as a sort of internal vision which we direct at experience in order to explore, understand and enlarge it. It is not intended to cover such deliberate problem-solving processes as mathematics, mathematical logic and so on. These certainly have their validity and usefulness, but they can be used only after the first stage of thinking (perception) has taken place. In ordinary life this first stage is usually the more important one.

Summary

There is no one satisfactory definition of thinking, since most definitions are satisfactory at one level or other. The definition of thinking as 'mental activity' is correct, since it covers everything, but it is not very helpful. On the other hand a definition of thinking as 'logic and reason' is correct but covers only one aspect. The definition which will be used here is this: '*Thinking is the deliberate exploration of experience for a purpose.*' That purpose may be understanding, decision-making, planning, problem-solving, judgement, action and so on.

Thinking and information

The educational trinity is: knowledge, intelligence and thinking. Intelligence is an innate quality that may depend on genes, early environment or a mixture of the two. It does not matter. One day we may discover that what we regard as intelligence is simply the speed of processing within the brain, which gives an 'intelligent' person a larger scan over the same period of time. It may depend on the rate of destruction of a particular enzyme acting at a synaptic site in the neurone network. Thinking is the operating skill through which intelligence acts upon experience. More will be said later about the relationships between thinking and intelligence. Knowledge or information is the basic material handled by thinking.

It is true that at one extreme thinking is impossible without some information on the subject. At the other extreme perfect information would make thinking unnecessary. In between these two extremes both thinking and information are required.

In school subjects it is too often assumed that information is more important than thinking. Thinking is regarded only as a tool for assimilating information, classifying it and putting it into its proper place. Information is very much easier to teach than thinking. Information can be tested in examinations in an objective manner. Within a closed subject area information may indeed seem to replace thinking. Thinking may even seem to be mere guessing.

It is a common experience in the academic world to find people who are so well informed within their own speciality that they can be classed as brilliant. Outside that speciality, however, their ability is much less, for information can no longer be a substitute for thinking.

Always to aim at getting information is admirable, but to await perfect information is impractical. In the ordinary world decisions and actions have to be taken, and since the information is usually imperfect it has to be supplemented by good thinking.

The relationship between thinking and information can be considered in two situations. In the first situation it is possible to collect a great deal of information. In the second situation it is not possible to collect enough information. Where it is possible to collect information it is often felt that this collection is more important than thinking. As a result science has been almost wrecked by the development of statistics as an information generator. Statistics can seemingly generate an endless amount of information in direct proportion to the effort invested. It is supposed that eventually enough information will have been collected for an idea to emerge. The history of science shows otherwise. It shows that a person looking in a different way at information that already exists can come up with new concepts. The human mind is such that it cannot absorb pure data. Data become information only when they are looked at through the spectacles of an idea. Einstein looked at the data that had been seen through the Newtonian idea and by looking at them in a different way came to a different conclusion. The constant interplay between information and ideas cannot be neglected. Ideas are generated by the application of thinking to data. When we collect information we collect data that have been organized by the old ideas. To improve those ideas we need thinking, not just more information. Until recently we thought that dinosaurs had died out. Now it seems that far from disappearing the dinosaurs may have evolved into birds. This illustrates the interplay between information and ideas. So even when it seems possible to fill a field with information this should not exclude the necessity for thinking.

In the second situation it is not possible to fill the field with information. In almost all situations involving decisions, planning or action there is a need and a desire for more information. But that information cannot be obtained, or cannot be obtained in time. In a contemplative area like science, history or literature one can wait patiently for the information to be discovered, but in a practical situation this is rarely the case. Furthermore in practical situations a person is usually dealing with the future: what will happen if I do this? How will people react to this? If I do not act will the situation develop in this way? In order to deal with the future one has to think very hard to make the experience of the past (the only experience we can have) applicable and to design decisions and plans that can cope with a number of alternative situations. All this requires a good deal of thinking.

Textbook problems are usually closed-ended. This is to say there is a definite known solution and all the required information is provided (or has been provided in the past). Real life problems are more often open-ended. That is to say there is no one definite solution and much of the required information is missing.

It is best to remember that information is no substitute for thinking and that thinking is no substitute for information. There is a need for both.

Thinking and talking

Articulateness and fluency in talking very often masquerade as thinking. The ability to generate thoughts and to link them together in a coherent way obviously involves a degree of thinking skill, but in itself it is no more than a skill in linking together in a grammatical fashion a number of ideas. Language practice and an articulate home background develop a language facility. Quite often the thinking is rather poor, because the actual thinking skill has not been developed as highly as the language skill and thoughts are poured willy-nilly into the vacuum created by fluent expression. Skill in expression is no more than skill in expression.

It would be wrong to assume that a skilled language-user is a skilled thinker. It would be wrong to assume that a person poor in verbal expression is therefore poor in thinking. We need language in order to let other people know what we are thinking, but grammatical coherence is not of itself the same as thinking. It is difficult, even impossible, to assess the thinking of a person who is unable to express it in language, but that does not mean that he has no thinking skill. In thinking lessons a pupil whose language ability was low enough for him to be regarded as backward has often blossomed as a thinker.

Language is very dependent on background. It is possible that thinking skill is also dependent on background, but if so it seems to be so to a lesser extent. I have a collection of many thousands of children's drawings in the five-to-twelve age group. The difference between the visual expression of thinking (in the drawing) and the verbal expression of thinking (in the accompanying writing) is great. A child with poor language skills may still express a sophisticated concept in his drawing. A child has little access to words except in his parents' conversation and in his own reading, if he has the opportunity and inclination to develop this. Visually there is much more opportunity to examine the world around him – television, picture books and so on – since vision is not a skill that has to be learned like reading.

It used to be argued that thinking itself was not possible without a repertoire of language-based concepts; that language was the very stuff of thinking and not just the means of expression. Today there is less support for this view as a result of work which has shown that in deprived cultures thinking may be just as effective as in advantaged cultures, even though the expression of it may appear limited. Thinking does not have to take place in words. Nor are concepts limited by the availability of words to describe them. Thinking can take place in images and feelings which are quite definite but too amorphous to be expressed in words.

The relationship between talking and thinking is an important one because of the twin dangers mentioned earlier, assuming that a person who is deficient in talking skills must also be deficient in thinking skill and incapable of developing such skill, and mistaking fluent expression for skilful thinking. Both these dangers are to be found in schools. Quite rightly great emphasis is placed on verbal expression. This is as it should be, because communication is more important than anything else. But verbal skill by itself is not enough. Talking and writing are too often accepted as being the same as thinking. A coherent and fluent essay may show language skill but does not thereby show thinking skill. We should look beyond language skill and seek to develop thinking skill as well. We need both.

Thinking and language

Talking is the use of language. Language itself is the code system we have developed for dealing with the environment and with other people. Language gives us usable concepts. Language restricts us to traditional concepts. Language provides the handles with which we grasp the world. It is not surprising that on a linguistic or semantic basis the relationship between language and thinking has been an extremely close one. Indeed so close is it that there are many who still regard thinking as semantic manipulation and all errors in thinking as semantic mismanagement. There are two reasons for the close relationship between language and thinking. One reason is cultural; the other is physical.

Until quite recently all sophisticated thinking was in the hands of religious organizations and quasi-religious philosophers. Theirs was acknowledged as the higher form of thinking, since instead of dealing with the practical matters of day-to-day life it dealt with the very meaning and purpose of life itself. In short this higher form of thinking dealt with metaphysics. Since metaphysics describes nothing except itself it became an elaborate construction of language concepts. The interplay of any two concepts created a third concept and so on. The only validity was an internal one.

The logical consistency of the structure was taken to prove its worth. In such a situation logical consistency is the same as semantic consistency. This situation is well illustrated by the famous proof of God's existence given by St Anselm: 'God is perfect. Perfection must include existence. Therefore God exists.' The movement from the concept of God to that of perfection is automatic, since the concept of God has been set up to include perfection. We have also created perfection as a concept which brooks no deficiency, so a perfect being cannot be short of existence. This is an extreme example but it does show how our tradition of semantic thinking came about. When words are no longer a means of looking at something but the something itself, then thinking is but a semantic exercise. The St Anselm proof is not very different from the reasoning of a nine-year-old which went as follows:

'Can God do anything?'
'Yes of course.'
'Can he make a stone?'
'Yes, and anything else.'
'Can he make a heavy stone?'
'As heavy as he likes.'
'Can he make a stone so heavy that God can't lift it?'

Historically the Church and the law have been close and it is no surprise that the legal system is based on semantic definitions. This is a practical way of proceeding, especially when combined with case law and a jury system to give the needed flexibility. It is only today that the system is beginning to break down because such hard and fast definitions as guilt and responsibility seem incapable of dealing with gradations of psychiatric disorder or social deprivation.

The second reason for the semantic influence in thinking is not cultural but physical. The brain receives a continuous flow of data from the environment. The brain is so constructed that it allows these incoming data to form themselves into patterns, as described in a later chapter. (For a description of the actual mechanism of the brain as a self-organizing information system see *The Mechanism of Mind* 1969.) The patterns are ideas or concepts. The attention system in the brain is an integral part of the way it works; it is not something added to the system. The effect of all this is to parcel the environment (both internal and external) into definite chunks that are recognizable and usable. If we have a language system then a word gets attached to these chunks and we have a concept and its description. Our thinking now deals with these ready-made chunks of the environment. The chunks are a definite size. Data are no longer fluid and atomic. We can no longer assemble data as we want to get the information we need. Much of our thinking is now no longer directed at the environment but at the concepts themselves: to see if we can pick some data out of one concept and put them together with data from another concept; to see if one concept does include some data or not. The old syllogistic arguments were concept explorations.

'Man is mortal. Henry is a man. Therefore Henry is mortal.'

This does no more than explore what we mean by the concept 'man' and the concept 'Henry'. On exploration we find that 'man' includes the concept of mortality (surprise!) and that 'Henry' includes the concept of 'man'. This is a historical exploration of how the concepts came to be set up.

The concept of guilt includes a whole complex of personal responsibility, awareness of some rule system, virtue, conscience, wrong-doing and so on. If the only crime was 'to be found out', as so many people seem to think today, then the concept of guilt would be replaced by the simpler one of 'discovery'. But the whole ethic and basis of punishment might have to change, so interlocked do our concepts become. Similarly the concept of profit includes: capitalism, surplus, exploitation, investment, risk and so on.

Our academic institutions, probably because they were established by the ecclesiastical authorities, have much too great a respect for semantic thinking. There is also a more practical reason for this reverence. A person who directs his thinking at words rather than at what they describe always feels in control of the situation. There is no further data that he would like to have, his data can never be shown to be wrong or insufficient. So an academic sitting in an academic tower never need descend to examine the vagueness of the real world where complete data are impossible. Instead he examines the semantic consistency of the argument, the words themselves rather than the thoughts which the words so imperfectly convey. This leads to logic-chopping, nit-picking, nuns' knitting and all the metaphysical gymnastics that result. It is easy and it is done.

If, however, we ever reached the stage when we could visualize a complex industrial system with a feedback loop from production and sales to investment and incentive, then we could look at that and it would not matter whether we called it profit, incentive, energy, value reservoir or anything else. To do that we should need an imaging system more powerful, more flexible and less chopped up than language. That is still a long way off.

We do need, from time to time, to look at our concepts, our perceptions and our language. But it is a very bad mistake – for which our academic institutions are solely responsible – to equate semantic tidiness with thinking skill. We must look at what is being thought about and then think about this. We must not quarrel about the means of expression in order to score minor debating points.

Some time ago in Britain there was a bad miners' strike. A questionnaire was distributed to the general public. The majority answers to the questions were roughly as follows:

'Are you against inflation?' YES.

'Do large wage increases cause inflation?' YES.

'Is the wage increase demanded by the miners going to increase inflation?' YES.

'Are you against giving the miners this large increase?' NO.

It was said that this showed the logical inconsistency of the public. It showed nothing of the sort. The public realized that the strike had reached a position where there was no choice but to give in. But they were still against inflation and they still realized that large wage increases fuelled inflation. Would it have been logically consistent for them to have indicated the following views?

'We have no choice but to give in to the miners.'

'That means that we accept a large wage increase.'

'We know that increases inflation.'

'Therefore we are in favour of inflation.'

It is possible to be against inflation yet still accept the practical realities of a situation.

It could be said that the main obstacle to our development of a more effective thinking system has been our obsession with semantic thinking.

Thinking and feeling

There is a current belief among many that gut feeling is what really matters and that thinking is just messing around with words. This is based on the experience that so-called logical thinking can be used to prove any point of view. Both sides in an argument always have logic and God on their side. All this arises from our mistaken insistence that logical validity is enough. Since, with different starting perceptions, perfectly logical thinking can lead to contradictory conclusions, it is not surprising that there has been some disillusionment with thinking in favour of gut feeling.

Ultimately it must be feeling that matters most. Feeling is what makes a human being human. In the end it is to satisfy our emotions and values that we arrange our actions. It is this very importance of feeling that makes thinking so necessary. Feeling is too important to be used in an arbitrary, capricious or merely habitual manner. The purpose of thinking is to prepare something for us to feel about. Thinking arranges and rearranges perception and experience so that we may have a clearer view of things. It is this clearer view that then excites our feelings. Without thinking feeling is a tyranny.

A friend of mine was driving along a road in Malta when he saw a woman being knocked down by a car ahead of him. Perhaps it was a hit-and-run driver or perhaps the driver hadn't even noticed. My friend stopped his car to help the woman. Another driver came up and, seeing the parked car and the injured woman, jumped to a conclusion and, getting out of his own car, he hit my friend and broke his jaw. There was no doubt about the strength of the driver's feelings. Unfortunately his perception was faulty and had misdirected the feelings.

Feelings are a sort of action. The purpose of thought is to

prepare us for action. In the same way thought prepares us for feeling. Thinking does not mean a laborious calculation as to how much feeling is required, but an attempt to direct attention and clarify perception. Thinking should never attempt to direct feeling. Thinking should never attempt to be a substitute for feeling. The job of thinking is to clarify perception. Feeling is then the reaction to this clearer perception. The feeling may still be wrong, misplaced or exaggerated, but that is a much lesser danger than trying to abolish feeling.

In practice it is extremely difficult to think first and feel second. The overwhelming tendency is to feel first and then use thinking to back up and support the feeling. This tendency is so overwhelming that even the most intelligent pupils (and adults) express an instant feeling-based judgement and then use their thinking to back it up in an essay or discussion.

The very first step in teaching thinking must be to provide a by-pass to this instant judgement by requiring the thinker to direct attention to all the relevant and interesting points in the situation. Thus in addition to his natural feelings he directs attention to the other aspects. A nine-year-old girl was very upset because her long hair had been cut – at her own request. In a sulk she locked herself in her room. In the morning, to her parents' surprise, she emerged smiling and in good humour. She explained that in a thinking lesson at school she had been taught deliberately to look through all the plus and minus points in a situation and she had applied this process to her haircut. As a result she could see that it would make swimming easier and would have many other advantages, so she was happy about it. In this girl's case the technique helped her to use her thinking to explore the situation instead of just to back up her initial reaction. Feelings may change as a result of an enlarged perception.

We trust our feelings because we cannot see how they can be wrong. Feelings are, indeed, always right – but within the universe created by our perception at the time. Unfortunately it is very difficult for us to accept that our perceptions may be wrong. And even more difficult for us to accept that our perceptions may be limited.

Thinking and ego

Descartes's famous remark, 'I think therefore I am', is true in a pyschological sense as well as in a metaphysical one. We are our thoughts. What else is there in our ego except what we are thinking at the moment? There may be a stored accumulation of individual experience, there may be a self-image, which may include physical appearance, there may be emotions; but our thoughts are more central to our ego than all of these. With our thoughts we can watch all these things and watch ourselves. It is hardly surprising that the ego and thinking are almost inextricably intertwined.

Up to the age of ten or eleven a child's ego is separable from his thinking. He enjoys thinking. He enjoys playing with ideas. He is wrong so often that his security is not dependent on his being right. After the age of eleven thinking becomes very much part of the ego and self-image. A person is as good as his thinking. His status at school and his social standing depend on his thinking. The value system imposed by schools makes pupils put a high value on cleverness. In a survey I once carried out with school-children 48 per cent of the boys and 52 per cent of the girls valued being clever above anything else. For the boys the next choice was being rich (far behind with 22 per cent) and for the girls the next choice was being good-looking (chosen by 23 per cent).

It is difficult to say how much this ego-involvement with thinking is the result of competitive school pressures and how much it is due to adolescent insecurity. The result is the same. It becomes impossible to look objectively at thinking as a skill. It becomes impossible for a pupil to look at this thinking and say, 'My thinking wasn't very good on that, was it?' Instead he has to defend his thinking by insisting that he is right or refusing to think about a subject in which he is going to be at a disadvantage. One of the main purposes of teaching thinking is to try to break this deadlock and get pupils to look objectively at their thinking, much as a tennis player might look objectively at the performance of his backhand in a match he is playing.

Unfortunately the more able or more clever the pupil, the more dependent does his ego become on his cleverness or thinking ability. While others may be prettier or may excel at sport, the clever girl treasures her cleverness and cannot bear to be wrong.

Since the clever pupils are the ones who get into university and thereafter into positions of influence, this effect is an important one. The self-image continues to include the need to be right all the time and it becomes almost impossible to develop objectivity about thinking.

The ego problem is seen to arise with the most able pupils when they are doing group work during a thinking lesson. They complain that they do not like working in groups because the individual's ideas are lost in the general group output and they cannot show 'how good my idea was'. The need to shine and to preserve status is important. The need to be right all the time and the fear of being wrong also distorts thinking in favour of the ego. But more important than both these is the absolute refusal to accept that thinking may be limited. A person would much rather be proved wrong than be told that his thinking was all right but limited. At least you may be right on another occasion, but being limited implies an inadequacy that will never be put right. Since it is impossible to tell a person that his thinking is limited, it is very unlikely that anyone should be capable of saying this to himself. A person will never admit to himself that his thinking is superficial or shallow or that it could be improved. The result is a colossal conceit in all matters connected with thinking. Nor is the conceit proportional to the ability. In the case of more able thinkers the conceit increases at a much greater rate than the thinking skill, so that a person who might be twice as skilled at thinking as another would be four times as conceited about that skill.

The ego problem is a very difficult one to overcome in the teaching of thinking. Much depends on the teacher. The method is to try to separate thinking as a deliberate and even artificial skill from the ordinary thinking activity of the ego.

Thinking as a skill

It is difficult to define a skill except by saying, 'A skill is a skill.' We could say, 'A skill is an ability to perform effectively in certain circumstances,' but this does not say very much. It is perhaps better to illustrate skill by examples than to use a definition. Manifestly thinking is a skill in as much as thinking can be performed skilfully. It is, however, important to decide whether thinking is a *learnable* skill. That is to say: is thinking a skill that can be improved by practice and direct attention or is it an innate ability? If thinking is nothing more than the raw application of an innate intelligence that has been genetically determined, then there is little that one can do about it and little point in trying to do anything about it. But it becomes a different matter if innate intelligence has to be applied with a learnable skill called thinking.

When I was at Harvard I tried out some simple block-arranging problems on my academic colleagues. There was one particular problem with which a lot of them had difficulty. Many of them declared they couldn't do it and others took as long as eleven minutes to do it. With this problem it was easy to take the first step, then to go on to the second step and next to proceed to the third step. Then came the difficulty. It seemed impossible to proceed further. The problem-solvers knew that they were intelligent. They also knew that the three steps already taken were correct. So they made an effort to go further. This same problem given to an average group of schoolboys is usually solved in about thirty seconds. The schoolboys take the three steps and then, seeing they are not getting anywhere, go back to the beginning and play around a bit with the blocks. They then start off along a different track and solve the problem quite easily. The schoolboys are more able to go back to the beginning and start again because they are less convinced that their original steps were correct. They are also free from the intellectual pride that forced the academics to go forward rather than retrace their steps. The experiment was not an important one, except in so far as it showed a difference between intelligence as such and the practical operating skill of thinking. The schoolboys were not more skilful in thinking, since their change of approach was partly due to lack of confidence in the first approach, and perhaps to impatience. But the academics who were unable to change their approach seemed deficient in skill on this account.

The engine power of a car, the effectiveness of its brakes, its road-holding ability, the sensitivity of its steering are all part of its innate characteristics. But the skill with which a car is driven is something apart. A powerful car may be driven with little skill. A humble car may be driven with great skill. There is of course a connection between driving skill and the power of a car in as much as a *skilled* driver would do better in the powerful car than in the humble car. Innate intelligence or IQ can be compared to the intrinsic power of the car. The skill with which this power is used is the skill of thinking. Thinking is the operating skill through which innate intelligence is put into action. A high intelligence may be allied to a high degree of thinking skill, but this is not necessarily so. Conversely a more modest intelligence may be accompanied by a high degree of thinking skill.

We are apt to look at extremes and to claim that a person with a very low IQ could not possibly exhibit thinking skill. At the other extreme a person with a very high IQ must be an effective thinker. Even if this were so – which it is not – such an argument from extremes has little value when one is dealing with the middle ranges of intelligence and thinking skill. It is also common experience that a high IQ is not necessarily associated with a broad skill in thinking. Quite often a high IQ is narrowly focused in an academic manner. That is why in ordinary language we distinguish between 'wisdom' and 'cleverness'. Cleverness is more appropriate to a high IQ and wisdom is more appropriate to skill in thinking (though experience comes into it as much).

Two-finger skills

If thinking is indeed a skill, how is it that we do not acquire this skill in the normal course of events? We develop skill in walking by practice in dealing with the world around us. We develop skill in talking by communicating with the world around us. Surely we must develop skill in thinking by coping with the world around us? The answer is that we do. But we must distinguish between a 'full' skill and a two-finger skill.

Many people who teach themselves to type early in life learn to type with two fingers. This is because they do not set out to *learn* typing as such but to *use* typing in their work. With two fingers they can more quickly acquire a tolerable level of competence than if they tried to develop skill with all ten fingers. So they learn a two-finger skill, that is to say a level of skill adequate to cope with their immediate needs. Yet a girl who trains to be a typist can, within a few weeks, develop a much higher degree of touch-typing skill, or what we may call a 'full' skill. The typist has acquired the full skill by direct attention to learning the skill. The two-finger journalist has acquired skill in the course of dealing with a limited situation and his skill is only just sufficient to cope with that situation. The major disadvantage of skills acquired in certain situations is that they are capable of coping with that situation. Prejudice is a very effective thinking skill in coping with certain situations. Prejudice gives instant judgement and decision and quick reactions. It is only in a wider context that prejudice is seen as a failure of thinking skill. In the same way two-finger typing is a skill, and yet in a wider context it is a block to developing further skills. Similarly the academic idiom taught at schools and refined in universities is a sort of two-finger skill. It is excellent at coping with closed situations where all the information is supplied, but it is very inefficient in dealing with open-ended situations where only part of the information is given yet a decision still has to be made. The academic idiom is good for looking for the truth and delaying decision until sufficient research

has revealed that truth. But it is not good for pragmatic or operating decisions.

We cannot rely on skills developed in the natural course of
events unless the natural course of events has been especially rich
in a variety of situations both narrow and broad. As with the
typist, it might be better to make some deliberate effort to train
skills directly.

In the ordinary course of events children tend to use their personality as much as their minds when arguing. They tend to insist
on their own point of view and to shout down other points of
view. In a sense this is a two-finger skill, which they have developed in the natural course of events. After a deliberate attempt
to teach thinking directly as a skill the following changes have
been noticed by teachers.

More listening to other people and less talking across people
Less egocentricity
Thinking used as exploration instead of just to support or defend
a particular point of view
Less giggling or whispering
Less abuse and shouting down and more tolerance of other views
Use of thinking modes other than the purely critical
Knowing what to do instead of just waiting for an idea to arrive
Less wandering off into irrelevancy
More willingness to think about new subjects instead of dis-
missing them as ridiculous or irrelevant
More confidence

These remarks apply especially to thinking or discussing in
groups. The changes arise as much from practice in the group
situation and in the opportunity for 'thinking' as from the actual
structure of the lessons. Nevertheless a change in skill has been
observed.

Unnatural skills

We tend to feel that skills ought to be natural. This is because we feel that a skill is something about which we don't have to think consciously. We forget that many skills that eventually become 'natural' are not really natural at all but have had to be learned in a deliberate and artificial manner. There is nothing natural about riding a bicycle. There is a very unnatural and awkward phase. It is only later that the skill becomes natural. The same is true of swimming. We do not swim naturally. It is only when we know how that it comes to seem very natural. Skiing also seems natural after we have learned how, but in the beginning it is very unnatural since we have to be trained to do things that are quite the contrary of natural: to lean forwards instead of backwards when going down a slope; to lean outwards instead of inwards when going round a bend.

This unnatural phase in learning a skill creates a huge problem in the teaching of thinking as a skill. We know that thinking ought to be natural and we often claim that the natural (two-finger) skill in thinking is sufficient anyway. We are therefore very reluctant to go through an unnatural and artificial stage. Yet this stage may be necessary in order to create new habits and new ways of directing attention.

Skill and tools

You could line up some people and let them run a race. This would tell you which of those people, under those circumstances, ran the fastest. This is ordinary competitive assessment. You could take each of these people individually and time how fast he or she could run. This is individual assessment of ability. If you were to train some of the people they would run faster than they had done before training. Nevertheless there would still be differences because the training would develop the innate potential of their running ability. The next thing you could do would be to invent bicycles or roller skates. You would now find that the people using these devices would be very much faster than the others, no matter how great the natural ability of the others. You could then train people to develop skill in using the devices.

Mathematics is an obvious example of a system of devices which we have developed to carry out certain thinking activities. The devices are excellent and carry us very much further than our natural mathematical abilities ever could.

Similarly in teaching thinking as a skill we may make use of some artificial devices. For instance we can create the operation 'Consider All Factors' which we will call CAF. In thinking about a situation a person can be asked to do a CAF. This will seem unnecessary since he will claim that he was about to do that anyway. Yet experience shows the falsity of this claim.

A group of adult graduates were divided into two random halves according to the date of their birthday (odd and even groups). Each random half was asked to consider a question and decide whether or not they approved of the suggestion. One half was asked to consider the suggestion of dated currencies, in which a currency would bear the year of issue and would not necessarily have the same value as that of another year of issue (the exchange rate would depend on inflation). The other half was asked to consider the suggestion that marriage should be a five-year contract. Thirty-five per cent favoured the dated currency and 23 per cent favoured contract marriage. The questions were now switched over (neither group had known the suggestion given to the other group). But this time each group was asked to list very carefully the 'plus' points in favour of the suggestion and the 'minus' points against it. Following this procedure the percentage in favour of dated currency fell from 35 to 11 per cent. The percentage in favour of contract marriage rose from 23 to 37. Assuming the groups were randomly matched (sixty people in each group) the results suggest that the deliberate listing of plus and minus points made a marked difference. And yet each of the people involved would have *claimed* to have looked at the advantages and disadvantages of any suggestion. If this claim were true, then being asked to do so should have made no difference at all.

On one occasion I was teaching a group of thirty ten-year-olds and I asked them if it would be a good idea for each child to be paid a wage for coming to school. Each child put up his hand to indicate approval of the idea. I then asked the children, working in groups, to apply the technique that was being taught in that lesson: to find 'plus', 'minus' and 'interesting' points about the idea. (They had been practising this technique on different situations throughout the lesson.) They did so: 'The bigger boys would attack us and take the money'; 'We would be charged for things and end up no better'; 'Our parents wouldn't give us presents but expect us to buy our own'; 'There would be problems deciding how much to give to different ages'; 'Where would the money come from?' and so on. When the original suggestion was again put to the class only one out of the thirty still approved. The other twenty-nine had changed their minds.

The nature of skill in thinking

Skill in thinking is a broad skill like skill in woodwork: knowing what to do, when to do it, how to do it, what tools to use, the consequences, what to take into consideration. It is much more than knowing the rules of logic or learning how to avoid logical errors. Skill in thinking has much to do with perception and with attention-directing. It is a matter of exploring experience and applying knowledge. It is knowing how to deal with situations, one's own ideas, the thoughts of others. It involves planning, decision-making, looking at evidence, guessing, creativity and very many other aspects of thinking.

For example the first batch of thinking lessons may set out to develop some skill in broadening perception. The intention is to encourage pupils to look more broadly at a situation instead of considering it only in terms of the egocentric and the immediate. The effect of these lessons on the pupils' thinking is indicated in the 'Results' section of this book. It seems clear that the lessons do help the pupils to think more widely. Whereas untrained pupils make an initial judgement and then generate only points that support that judgement, trained pupils are able to generate points that oppose their own view as well as those that support it.

The aim is to produce a 'detached' thinking skill so that the thinker can use his skill in the most effective way. A thinker ought to be able to say, 'My thinking on this is not very good,' or, 'My thinking performance is poor in this area,' without feeling that his ego is threatened.

An example
of thinking in action

Two groups of children aged ten to eleven from a rural school discussed the suggestion that children should be paid a weekly wage for going to school. There were five children in each group and the discussions were tape-recorded. A transcription of both recordings is given here. In the transcription there are gaps (indicated by dots) where noise or confusion of voices made transcription impossible. One group had done ten thinking lessons with a very good teacher. The other group had not done any and are called the 'control group'.

Tone

The transcript contains comments like 'screaming' or 'shouting' but it is impossible to convey the tone of the discussion. The control group tended to shout each other down and to emphasize a point by shouting. There was a particularly large amount of shouting in the voting episode. In addition there were giggling and whispering and general fooling around, as might be expected. Such things are obvious only if one can listen to the tape itself. The content of thought and the style of thinking are, however, apparent in the transcript.

This group had done the first ten thinking lessons:

If they get paid they'd be sort of taking advantage wouldn't they?

Why should they get paid?

Because they're learning something. It's going to help them. It's going to help them to get paid when they grow up.

You see, their fathers they all go to work and they'll say, 'Well, if our children are getting so much they may get higher than us,' and the fathers'll go on strike.

Anyway children don't appreciate money very well, do they? They'll spend it any old how . . . sweets.

If they did get paid . . .

Yes, but then the school could go on strike.

How could school go on strike?

Not give the children enough money. Yea – pocket money.

Why sh . . . the children aren't going to work really are they?

They're just . . . nice information . . . the teachers are . . . must do . . .

They [can be] like some children now. They just sit in the class and don't work.

Look, say we get . . .

Yea.

Look, the teachers are teaching and we're getting paid for while they're teaching. They might not have enough money to pay the teachers. Where are they going to get all the money from?

Who'll pay?

The teachers.

The [school].

And it can't keep coming out of the taxpayers' money.

And if you were trying to get a minibus like us would go to the minibus and that'd just be a waste.

Yea, but the money would just go down the drain.

The children would just buy sweets and stuff.

The teachers would go on strike in future and there may be no schools to teach.

If the children are . . .

They'll be leading the world.

And if you were trying to get a minibus like us the money would go to the minibus and that'd just be a waste.

That'd only appeal to a few schools and everybody'd start crowding those schools and they couldn't teach properly.

If the first-years, third-years, second-years and fourth-years all got the same money then fourth-years will all get cross and say, 'We need more money than the first-years because we're learning harder.' Then they get more money. Then the first-years will say, 'No, we need more money,' and it'll be gradually higher up the scale. Yea.

Actually they should do the same work each then, if they did have money it would be the same each.

Hm. I don't think there should be money at all.

It's really a waste of money actually.

'Cos, they aren't doing any work to help anybody.

They're not going to help anybody 'cept their parents.

We're just going to help teachers . . . children.

Yea, but if children get paid their parents . . . that means taxes'll go up.

Yes, they get paid.

If they're in a rented house the taxes go up and then, because they've got more money –

And the wages of the parents'll come down . . . and then for . . . Say your dad works in a factory or something.

Yes, like a highly expensive one.

Your dad has to have his wages down.

But there might be another man there who hasn't got any children to get paid so his wages go down as well won't they?

That's true . . .

. . .

Well, let's see, they, if they get paid, they'll have some of the money, and they'll bring things to school.

They can easily lose the money if they get paid.

If we do pay children they'll just come to school and sit there, and they won't do nothing, they'll just come for the money.

Like us. When we are with Mrs S. We just talk then we'd just get money for doing hardly nothing.

Be a waste of money.

We just read, get information from books which the school buys or we'd just be sitting there, which is not work.

I would say that if we do get paid . . . some money . . . If you do want to get paid you should work hard.

If you do want to get paid only people who work hard should get paid.

No, if you want to get money your parents, when you first come to school, should pay about £20 to £50, which'll pay for all your wages.

But you see, Tony, well really, when you go swimming you're not helping no one, are you?

That's not really worth having.

There's some private schools, like London, and they pay so much a term, and if we start paying it'll bring the country down, 'cos that's what England's really for – National Health Service, and everything. So if you do put prices on things like that you wouldn't call this a primary school, you'd call it a private school.

It's a bad idea right from the beginning really.

It'll never turn out right.

Well, and you'd take advantage of it too ... stay on in school longer.

The schools in England, they'll be going down and down and down. There won't be many left because the ones that want to build more extensions on to their school they need more money, so they're giving their money away to the children.

They'll stay on at school just for the money.

And the school will get smaller actually.

The next transcript is from the group who had not done any thinking lessons.

Yes.

Starting now. Yea, we should, shouldn't we?

I should. If we go to school I reckon we should get paid for one reason.

Why should we work for the teachers?

If we didn't work ... education –

Yea, but if we didn't work they wouldn't get paid [*giggle*] Why should they get paid and not us?

Go on strike.

If we didn't go to school, none of us went to school –

They get paid, why shouldn't we?

I don't see why the teachers get as much holidays as we do.

We do things like collage. They don't. They don't do nowhere near as much as us. Do they though?

We might get about 10p a week.

No, 50.

No, if we do get money 50 is going a bit too far.

We should have free school dinners.

And milk.

Even if we are over seven, we should still get milk.

We always used to.

'Cos that makes you strong and healthy.

[*whisper*] We're supposed to be talking about . . . not milk.

What will we do with the money when we get it though?

Put it in me money-box and save up for the holidays.

I'm going to spend it on sweets.

You get . . .

Well, I reckon they have far too much holiday, and we don't get enough.

No, the teachers get far too much though.

Yea, but why should they get paid and we not?

We [should only] spend 10p for school dinners.

Yea, we're the ones that do the work.

I say that teachers have to work as well. They have to explain what we do.

I don't see what the teachers are moaning about. They get enough holidays but we should go on strike.

Why?

If we don't get paid.

Why should they go on strike?

They're not [*screaming*]. I know, but –

Teachers do go on strike.

Only sometimes.

They have in London.

They have nothing to moan about though. They have far more holidays than any other paid workers and they um . . .

I think it would be a good idea if we had a bit more holiday.

Yea, but why should they . . .

Because if they do we can . . .

About eight months.

No really ... like ... Wednesday every week we should have a holiday.

We should have every three weeks holiday, every three [weeks]
You should really come to school on Saturday, I reckon, as well.
What for [*screaming*]?
I don't ... I don't ...'cos I'd miss Jerry Lewis then.
So what?
At least you'd get a good job when you grow up.
[*whisper*] ...
We supposed to be talking ...
I don't think –
What are you whispering about?
I don't think it would be a good idea if you had money really.
What's the point?
We're supposed to go to school. Money's only bits of paper anyway.
And bits of silver and gold.
It's better to be clever than earning a lot of money, ain't it?
The teacher should be given and not –
It's better to be brainy than have wood in your head.
True! True!
Anyway the school dinners go up too much.
Yea, they're always going up.
Last ... right ... (*shouts*) No, no!
Last year they were 5op now it's 6o.
Yea, yea, I'll tell you something. Yea, we should get money.
I don't think it would be a good idea because we're supposed to go to school. We shouldn't really have money really.
I don't think so.
Yea, we should, shouldn't we? We should [*shouts*] we should.
What's the point?
We can buy sweets every day when we come home from school.
Yea, and buy a portable TV.
Yea, that'll be great won't it [*shouting*]?
The teachers should give us tuppence every day.
Make it 5.
No 2p every day.
No, I don't think –

We should get money.

Two pence.

I reckon we should be allowed to chew sweets in school as well.

You would!

Why? I don't think we should.

I reckon we should.

We *should*.

We should have money.

What's the point? What would you do with the money?

[*shouting*] Spend it!

Save it! Save it!

What me and Graham are going to do when we're about sixteen, we're going to buy a boat –

Oh, a boat [*laughter*].

That's what I'm going to save up for.

I want to buy a horse.

A horse?

No, we should really be grateful for the money we do get.

We don't get any.

We should be grateful for free lessons anyway.

Free lessons?

Yea, free without paying any money.

A long time ago you used to get the cane if you'd done anything wrong then.

We still do . . . [*laugh*] . . . Mr Petting.

Do you reckon it's worth going to school though?

No.

Yes.

No.

How long do you reckon you should have off in a year, in a whole year?

Summer holiday six weeks, Easter holiday fortnight – should be about four weeks.

[*whisper*] What's that got to do with the money?

Money quiz [*laughter*]. If we eat Marathons . . .

There's a competition on tonight.

Shh [*laughter*].

That's . . .

Miss Simpson said we had very good ideas last time. Anyway we got good ideas this time.

Look –

Do you reckon teachers get enough money or not?

Yea, they get too much, double what we'd let them have.

If they gave everyone 5p a week, though, they wouldn't have any money left would they?

Yes, they would. They'd have about a hundred quid.

I think that if we did our lessons well, you know, and if we'd done a good week's work, I think we should get money then. If we don't do our work properly, if we muck about like you do (like ...) and Kerry McCoggin, then we shouldn't get money.

Only the brainiest.

Yea.

No.

No.

The ones that work well like me ...

The person who's Miss should give a packet of sweets to the person who's ...

No. Money's best.

About 2p.

2p.

Yes.

...

And we should be allowed to eat gum in school.

He's already chewing gum [*giggle*].

Well, we're not really meant to, so ... [*whispering*] ...

Hey, why should we?

I don't see why we don't get paid.

There's no point in it.

Say Yes. If we all vote that we should get paid –

Yes, yes, yes.

No.

Great. It's four against one. You're ... you're outvoted ...

Do you think we should get paid?

Yea. Two quid a week.

Do you?

No ... do you?

Yea.

So do I.

So I reckon that we should.

[*repeated shouting*] WE WANT MONEY!

Why don't the teachers not get paid and we have the money?

[*whispering*] Kevin, how much more time have we got?

Oh, come on, let's hurry. Shut up.

Yea, well we should get paid.

Yea, I reckon we should.

We should get paid at least 2p.

Yea, when this is over we ring and tell Mr P. We need 2p a week.

I reckon we should have free milk.

Free milk, and free dinners.

It shouldn't be seven when we don't get milk either. It should go up to at least fourteen.

The trained group

The general arguments used by this group run as follows:

Why should children get paid? They are learning things which are going to benefit them when they grow up.

Where is the money going to come from? There might not be enough money to pay teachers. There might not be enough money to build school extensions. The money could be better spent elsewhere – for instance on the minibus the school is trying to buy.

The required money would have to come from the taxpayers and you can't go on increasing taxes. The wages would go down and this would be unfair on someone who didn't have any children who were being paid at school.

Children don't appreciate money and they would spend it on sweets.

Some children just sit in class and do no work. Swimming is not helping anyone and so why should children get paid for it? Some children would take advantage of the system and just stay longer in school to get more money.

There might be problems in deciding how much money each school year should receive.

If only a few schools tried it they would get overcrowded very quickly.

Perhaps you could get paid only if you worked very hard. Perhaps your parents could pay a deposit from which the child would get paid if he worked hard. But this might make it more like a fee-paying private school.

Summary

Children do not deserve to get paid for going to school, and where would the money come from?

Control group

The general arguments used by this group run as follows:

If teachers get paid so should pupils. The pupils work harder than the teachers.

Teachers get paid too much and they are always moaning and even going on strike.

Teachers get too many holidays and the pupils want more holidays. Discussion on length of holidays and suggestions for holidays.

Complaint about the price of school meals and discussion on free school milk.

The money could be spent on sweets, a horse, a boat, portable television and so on.

Children should be allowed to chew sweets in school.

A vote will show if the idea is a good one and whether children deserve to be paid for going to school.

Summary

Teachers get paid so children should get paid too.

General comparison

The control group showed a tendency to drift off the subject in what can be called 'point-to-point' thinking. A point which comes up in an argument provides the starting point for a new line of thinking or a new discussion area, even if this is irrelevant to the main topic. For example, it was mentioned that money could be saved for a holiday and this led on to mention of teachers' holidays and then to consideration of holidays in general with complaints and suggestions in this area. The claim that children worked was countered with the statement that teachers worked and this was followed by a comment that they were always moaning and this led to a consideration of teachers' strikes (topical at that time). There was talk about buying sweets with the money; about giving sweets instead of money to those who worked hardest and about freedom to chew gum in school. Once school milk was mentioned it had to be discussed as a subject in its own right. There was no mention at all of where the money would come from to pay the pupils or whether they deserved it. The thinking seemed to be on an adversary basis, with one person trying to convince another of his views and in this respect voting was used as the final arbiter.

In contrast the trained group seemed to be exploring the subject rather than fighting about. They kept more closely to the subject without branching off into other subject areas.

Contrast: 'Look the teachers are teaching and we're getting paid for while they're teaching. They might not have enough money to pay the teachers. Where are they going to get all the money from?' with: 'Why should they [the teachers] get paid and not us?'

Errors in thinking

Our traditional approach to the teaching of thinking is based on the dangerous fallacy that error-free thinking is good thinking. And by errors we mean logical errors. We have considered it sufficient to demonstrate the different types of logical error and to criticize them when they arose. With our more successful pupils the result has been our highly esteemed error-free academic thinking. This has been held up as the goal of all training in thinking. The perfection of this form of thinking rests on three things: fluency; freedom from error; logical consistency. Fluency arises from articulateness and a large repertoire of idioms, concepts and referral material. Fluency as such has very little to do with skill in thinking and much too often masquerades as such. Freedom from error means freedom from visible error; this is not only inadequate as a criterion of skilful thinking but positively dangerous, since an argument that is free from visible error is taken to be correct when in fact it may be quite wrong, as we shall see later. In a similar manner logical consistency or internal validity is insufficient and dangerously misleading. There are many logically consistent arguments that are based on unacceptable value systems or inadequate perception.

It is relatively easy to define logical errors and to spot them. The next step is to assume that an argument which avoids these errors is valid. It is very much more difficult to define skilful thinking in a positive manner, and so we have relied on detecting and avoiding errors.

Everyone would agree that logical errors make for bad thinking. But we are completely unjustified in assuming the opposite: that freedom from logical error makes for good thinking. A faulty computer will give the wrong answers. A faultless computer will not give the right answers: it will only give answers that are consistent with the data it has been given and the programme it is using. In the computer world there is a saying 'GIGO' which means 'Garbage in, garbage out'. The excellence of the computer, like the excellence of logic, cannot make up for deficiencies on the input side. The fact that a car is being driven with great skill does not mean that it is on the right road or even going in the right direction. It may also have missed an important turning.

A photographer takes a picture of a river for a competition. The panel of judges examine the photograph and decide that the trees are too purple in colour and that not enough of the river can be seen. They can tell these things by looking at the photograph. They are looking for internal validity. But they cannot tell that the photographer was trying to include a flock of geese that were passing overhead, but failed to do so. Nor can they tell that he removed from the negative an ugly electricity pylon that wrecked the scene.

In practical life very few errors in thinking are logical errors. Most thinking is free from visible and logical inconsistencies. The errors are not so much errors as inadequacy of perception. And these inadequacies of perception cannot usually be detected by internal examination of the thinking. That is why our assumption that error-free thinking is valid has been so very dangerous. Any inadequacy of perception is not only accepted but endorsed, provided it is treated thereafter with logical consistency.

Our obsession with logical error has not only failed to deal with the major causes of poor thinking but has prevented us from paying attention to those causes. As noted earlier, this obsession is easily explained. We can see and define logical errors very neatly; they are tangible and noticeable. We equate thinking with mathematics and treat errors in the same way. Finally our thinking traditions are based on ecclesiastical traditions, especially the Thomist insistence on Aristotelian logic. In the metaphysical world such an emphasis is of course vital, since logical validity is the only validity. In the real world, however, we have to cope with what is, rather than with what we have constructed in our minds.

We can now look at some of the major errors in thinking. It can be seen that very few of them can be called logical errors unless one extends the meaning of the word 'logic' to mean all effective thinking, in which case any deficiency is automatically an error in logic. Such an extension would make the word useless.

Partialism

This is by far the major error in thinking and it is a pure error of perception. It is an inadequacy or insufficiency of perception. The thinker is looking at only part of the situation and basing his argument on that part. It is an error that is consistently and deliberately used by politicians or by anyone else who has to make a point. Indeed it is the easiest way to make a point, since by carefully choosing an area one can build a logically consistent argument and then rely on the logic of that argument to carry the point.

A trade-union leader insists that his men need a large wage rise to cope with the rising cost of living. His argument is correct when looked at in terms of his men and the cost of living. But on a larger scale the wage rise will be paralleled elsewhere and will itself lead to a further rise in the cost of living. The manufacturer insists that his selling price must be four times the cost of the materials that go to make up the item. So if the price of raw materials increases, his selling price and profits increase proportionately, although his other costs have not increased. He has chosen to look at his usual pricing procedure, not at the change in raw-material costs or the effects of his price increase.

Often the partialism is intentional. Sometimes it may be very difficult to detect unless one knows the whole situation. It may be absolutely impossible to detect by internal examination of the argument. At other times the partialism is unintentional and is based on inadequate information. If the information is equally inadequate all round, then the 'error' will never be detected.

A police force adopts some new procedures. The following year there is a rise in the crime rate of 12 per cent. It is argued that since the measures were intended to bring down the crime rate the measures have been a failure. This seems logically consistent. But it involves partialism and inadequate perception. We should like to know what the rise in crime rate was the previous year. We find that it was a mere 8 per cent. So it seems that the new measures have been followed by an even steeper increase. Surely they must be ineffective? But do we know what the rise in crime rate would have been without the measures? It might have been 24 per cent. Do we know what has been happening in other comparable countries?

Time-scale

This is a special case of partialism in which a person looks at a narrow slice of time – usually the immediate future. A schoolboy wants to leave school because his friends who have left school earlier are earning a lot of money. He argues that since the purpose of school is to train him to earn a living it would be logical for him to leave if he could earn a good living. The teacher tries to persuade him that further education would benefit him later on in life and enable him to earn more money later.

Obviously the teacher's perception and the boy's are not the same. Both are arguing correctly, but from a different time-scale of perception. This is an especially difficult area because a choice of time-scale can make all the difference to an argument. And who is to say which time-scale is the most appropriate? The way out of this problem is to insist that the thinker should be able to extend his perception over the whole time-scale and then having done this choose which time-scale he wishes to apply to the situation. For instance if the schoolboy had been able to see what the teacher saw and still argued that he preferred immediate earnings to years of study and delayed earnings then his perception would have been sufficient, even though his value system or logic might have been at fault.

Egocentricity

Narrow-band thinking or tunnel vision in pupils is usually based
on egocentricity. They see a situation only in terms of how it
affects them personally. The partial area of perception is firmly
centred on themselves. Egocentricity is justified in the sense that
the personal purpose of thinking is to benefit oneself by enabling
one to cope more effectively with the world. As suggested before,
the error lies not so much in looking after one's own interests but
in being unable to see the rest of the situation. If one is able to see
a wide field and then returns to consider the matter in egocentric
terms, that is different from being able to see only the egocentric
part of the field. In the trade-union example, a wider field of vision
might show that even in egocentric terms asking for a large wage
rise does not make sense. In teaching thinking skill one is not
trying to teach morals. Egocentric partial perception is wrong in
terms of thinking skill. A person who could expand his perception
but still returned to follow the egocentric approach might be correct in his thinking, though selfish in his morals. But to be unable
to see further is just poor thinking.

Arrogance and conceit

These constitute a very common and very important error in
thinking. It is not only impossible to detect on the 'logical error'
basis but is made much worse by this sort of examination. The
conceit error arises when there is an apparently logical explanation for something and this is then taken to be the *right* explanation. The logical consistency of the explanation seems to confer
validity on it. The error lies in the fact that this satisfaction with
the explanation prevents any search for other explanations. After
all, if one has a logically correct explanation why should one
search further? Yet there may be other explanations that are just
as good or even better. There is no logical way of proving that

there must be other explanations beyond the first one. For this reason this is a very difficult error to overcome. You cannot insist on someone looking further than he is inclined to look. You cannot show any good reason why he should look further in any particular case, though in general you might be able to make a case for his doing so. The result is that in many cases proof is often no more than lack of imagination. We have a logical explanation that fits the facts – we cannot imagine any other explanation – so we accept the explanation as proved. New methods of teaching reading are introduced. The reading standards fall. Logically the fall must be due to the new methods of teaching. It is difficult to insist on someone going beyond this explanation to consider, for instance, whether many hours spent watching television might be reducing reading time or interest. In my book *Practical Thinking* I called this error the 'Village Venus effect', on the basis that in a remote village the prettiest girl would be considered to be the most beautiful girl in the world, because no one would be able to imagine a girl more beautiful until such a girl had been sought and found.

This particular type of error is very important for two reasons: first, because it does not seem to be an error at all and hence there is no way of getting a person to look further; second, because in most situations there is usually an apparently logical way of coping and this pre-empts any search for a better way. It could be said that the advance of science has been due solely to those scientists who were emotionally equipped to be dissatisfied with the current explanation and to seek better explanations. This is by no means a natural property of mind. Very rarely does logical inconsistency in the current explanation force us onwards. On the contrary apparent logical consistency reinforces our arrogance and conceit.

Initial judgement

This is a second major source of error in thinking and one which is actively encouraged in schools. It occurs at all levels of thinking, even among the most brilliant people. A proposal is presented. The thinker makes an initial judgement as to whether he likes or dislikes the proposal. Thereafter he uses his thinking skill and logical powers to back up his initial judgement. The thinking is not used to *explore* the situation and then to arrive at a judgement. It is used to support a judgement that has already been made on the grounds of prejudice, emotion, belief, social grouping and so on. Unfortunately this habit is encouraged in some schools, which train pupils to write down their views in the first line of the essay and then to use the rest of the essay to support that position.

Our whole system of adversary thinking in politics, in the courts, in school debates is based on the logical support of a position. It is assumed that if a position is logically supportable then it must be right. Unfortunately it is possible to have mutually contradictory positions, each of which is logically supportable if the value systems and perceptions are different.

We see no harm in making initial judgements because we believe that it is the logical support of that position that really matters. Naively we believe that if logical support cannot be mustered then the judgement will be changed. Of course this never happens, because the skilled logical mind can create consistent arguments to support virtually any point of view. Indeed it is our very insistence on the importance of logical argument that makes it necessary for us to rush to initial judgement. If we did not make such initial judgements what would our logic have to work on? It is only if we are trained to put a process of *exploration* in place of *logical support* that we can examine a situation and extend our perception of it. Exploration opens up perception, whereas logical support closes it down by eschewing those areas which do not offer the required support.

It is a characteristic of the mind that if it does not have something else to do it will form a judgement. Judgement is the same basic process as recognition and identification, which are the fundamental processes of our pattern-making and pattern-using minds. Judgement goes a little further than mere recognition by including an emotional element ('I like it' or 'I do not like it') or a projection-in-time element ('It will work' or 'it won't work'). Judgement also allows for the application of any prejudice or preexisting bias. Indeed so basic is the initial judgement process that the very first of the thinking lessons is concerned with providing a bypass to judgement.

Adversary thinking

As suggested above, our adversary tradition in thinking puts the emphasis on logical support of positions rather than on mutual exploration. A politician will strive towards what is different in his position from his opponents', rather than move towards what is mutually agreed. This makes for polarization. Because the emphasis has shifted from exploration to logical support, we get the additional phenomenon whereby validity for one argument can be obtained by showing a logical error in the adversary argument: 'You are wrong – therefore I am right.' This is a truly ridiculous situation. The logical error of someone else's argument shows nothing beyond the logical error of that argument. It cannot in any way validate the opposing argument. They might both be wrong. It is a supreme arrogance to assume that there are only two, sharply polarized, positions on an issue and that if one is wrong the other must be right. On that basis all you need to do to prove the validity of your argument is to find a logically weak person to defend the opposite argument. Ridiculous as it is, this is a very common procedure.

Ego-involvement

The need to be right at all times is a more powerful objective than most in determining the direction of thinking. A person will use his thinking to keep himself right and then believe whatever position that thinking has generated. This is especially true with more able pupils, whose ego has been built up over the years on the basis that they are brighter than the other pupils. Such a person finds it very difficult to admit a mistake and almost as difficult to acknowledge the value of someone else's idea. Thinking is no longer used as an exploration of the subject area but as an ego-support device. Thinking is used to support the ego, just as it is used to support an initial judgement. The objectivity required in truly skilful thinking is completely lacking. Yet the arguments that result may be brilliantly logical and consistent.

The basic problem is that we normally regard logic as a way of processing our perceptions and extracting the full implications from them. We fail to notice that in many situations, such as ego-support, the logical structure comes first and has its own momentum, and perceptions are tailored to fit that structure. Inevitably, in skilled hands, the structure is consistent but the perceptions are woefully partial.

Magnitude error

Traditional logical systems have great difficulty in dealing with magnitude, because language deals with the nature of something rather than its size. The great philosopher Descartes had a long argument with Harvey over the circulation of the blood. Descartes insisted that the heart heated up the blood and that this propelled it round the body. Heating fluid does cause expansion, but not nearly enough to act as a pumping force. Unless one actually *knows* the magnitudes involved it is easy to construct an apparently logical argument' which is nonsense. It is in this respect that the magnitude error is one of the other major errors in thinking, for it is an error of perception.

Consider the advertising claim: 'Antiseptics kill germs. Germs act on decaying food to cause mouth odour. If you use an antiseptic mouthwash you will have fresher breath.' This all seems very logical. But the magnitudes are quite wrong. The antiseptic is diluted so quickly in the mouth that it will kill germs for only a minute at the most. Germs multiply so quickly that they will replace themselves very rapidly. In any case the concentration of antiseptic that will kill germs in a test-tube in the laboratory is very different from the concentration obtained in a mouthwash.

Similarly: 'Cars use petrol. So if everyone drove half as much as they now drive the oil-importing bill would be much reduced.' This seems logical enough, but the magnitudes show that the amount of oil used as petrol in cars is only a small fraction of the imported oil, most of which is used for heating or industry. So a reduction in motoring would lead to only a small reduction in imported oil.

As with other types of error mentioned in this section, the magnitude error is not detectable by examination of the argument itself. The argument may be logically consistent and internally valid. The error is detectable only if one already has a larger field of perception in which to judge the argument.

Extremes

Young children often argue from extremes. In discussing the question of immigration, children might complain that if immigration was made easy then 'Immigrants would flood in and soon they would take over all the jobs and all the people here now would starve.' In discussing the suggestion that bread, fish and milk should be made free the children would declare, 'Everyone would rush to the shops and there would be riots and soon the sea would be empty of fish.'

This type of argument occurs with adults as well. One teacher complained that teaching thinking might make pupils treat thinking as an objective skill; this would mean that they would not use their emotions and would therefore be a bad thing. Of course it would be. But one can stop well short of that point and yet develop an objective thinking skill which is used in conjunction with feeling. The same type of extreme argument is used to discuss the relationship between thinking skill and IQ. It is suggested that people with a very low IQ cannot be skilled in thinking and that people with a very high IQ must be intelligent enough to have developed a skill in thinking. Both these things may be true (though not necessarily), but this does not mean that in between there is a constant relationship between thinking skill and IQ.

To some extent the extremes habit arises from our custom of dealing with absolute concepts and definitions. Once something has entered the definition box it is treated as similar to everything else in that box. So if we can argue that thousands of dogs in a town would be a bad thing that means that dogs in general would be a bad thing, and then that individual dogs, as dogs, are a bad thing, quite irrespective of the total number in the town. In our classification system a table is a table. Yet in some circumstances a small table may be useless and in others a large table may be equally useless. In practice we accept this. 'I hear you're moving into a new house so I'm going to give you a table' would not be acceptable unless the receiver were to look at the table before accepting it. Yet in practice we often construct logical arguments in which the magnitude of an effect is disregarded. Pupils discussing a suggestion for weekend prisons for minor offenders dismissed the idea on the grounds that the prisoners would run away during the week and not return to the prison. Logically this is correct. Some would undoubtedly run away, but would the numbers be so large as to make the scheme unworkable? How large is large? How long is a piece of string?

Summary

The three basic types of error discussed in this section are all based on inadequacies of perception. None of them is detectable as a logical error in the traditional sense. None of them will alter the internal validity of an argument. Yet in practice these errors are far more important than the traditional logical errors. They are more important not only because they occur more often but because they occur even in the case of the most able thinkers, who manage to avoid logical errors without difficulty. Furthermore the traditional emphasis on logical validity can dangerously endorse arguments that are logically valid but perceptually inadequate. By emphasizing the gravity of logical error we appear to prove the validity of an argument that is free from such error. That is the real danger.

In many of the instances quoted above it may seem that what is called perceptual inadequacy is really ignorance or lack of knowledge. It may be said that no one should be blamed for the deficiency of an argument that has to be based on currently available knowledge rather than on absolute knowledge. This is true. But perception is not the same as knowledge. Perception is the way we look at available knowledge and the way we direct attention over available knowledge. The faults lie not so much in the inadequacy of knowledge but in the inadequacy of the way we look at it. If we look at a situation only in an egocentric manner that is because we choose to do so. If we arrogantly assume that a plausible explanation excludes all others that is because we choose to do so.

The purpose of this section is to demonstrate that freedom from logical error is not the same as thinking skill. Our traditional adoption of this fallacy has made it difficult to develop broader thinking skills, and especially to recognize the huge importance of perceptual skill in thinking.

Perception, logic and thinking

The teaching of thinking is *not* the teaching of logic but the teaching of perception. At various places in this book it will be obvious that I wish to make this point very strongly. There is a need to make the point strongly. Our traditional approach to the teaching of thinking as a skill has concerned itself almost exclusively with the teaching of logic. Logic, and especially Aristotelian logic, has played an important part in our culture for centuries. This has come about both as a result of the classics tradition but even more as a result of the way St Thomas Aquinas repackaged Aristotle and so provided the Scholasticism that determined the thinking of the Church and the whole education system which the Church then controlled. Logic is tangible and direct. We can make rules and observe mistakes. It almost has the neatness and formality of mathematics. Whenever anyone sets out to teach thinking there is a strong temptation to drift back into teaching logic, because this seems to be the only definite thing that can be taught.

In its proper place logic is a tool of perception. It is perhaps most important in metaphysical arguments which involve words and concepts. The role of logic is to show what is implicit in the concepts used and to expose contradictions. Logic has a similar role in disputes and arguments where it is used in an attempt to show the contradictory nature of the opposing argument. It still has a role to play in the sort of thinking that deals with real situations rather than with words, but the role is less dominant.

The purpose of a jury is to 'see clearly' the situation of a crime. They have to 'think' about it. They have to explore the experience of the crime. The experience is given to them in raw chunks by the witnesses as evidence. The role of the lawyer is to *direct the attention* of the jury to certain aspects of the evidence. Having drawn their attention to some part of the evidence, the lawyer may help them to enlarge their perception of this part. Finally he may use logic to make explicit what is implicit in this special piece of evidence. Logic is used as a tool to make explicit what is implicit – but cannot easily be seen by a process of directing attention to an area.

We use mathematics in order to 'see clearly' what is implicit in a set of relationships which we have been given. There is no way in which we can direct attention which will make explicit what is implicit. So we go through a mathematical procedure in order to process the situation so that we may see it more clearly. In most ordinary thinking, however, we can do a great deal by directing attention before moving into the processing stage.

Quite often embarking in too great a hurry on the processing stage of thinking (logic) can limit our exploration in the attention-directing stage.

'The police break into a locked flat. They find John and Mary dead on the floor. They are naked and are lying in a pool of water. The window is open and there is broken glass on the floor. What has happened?' The mind races away to construct scenarios of crime which will accommodate all the evidence. In fact the explanation is quite simple. John and Mary are pet goldfish. The cat got in through the open window and upset the goldfish bowl – hence the glass and water on the floor. Goldfish are always naked. This unfair trick question illustrates how rushing into processing can limit perceptual exploration.

A small town has a traffic-congestion problem. There are parking spaces in the shopping area but these tend to become occupied by commuters who leave their cars there all day rather than by the short-term shoppers for whom they are provided. How could one tackle the problem? I have given it to many professional problem-solvers. They all choose meters and then work out meter-charge schemes which escalate with time or give some 'time-up' indication. This is a satisfactory approach. Another approach is to say that cars can park where they like without any charge or meter – but they must leave their headlights on. This ensures short parking times since each driver will be conscious that he is running down his battery. Once the mind has settled on meters then there is nothing else to do except to work out charges. Here again rushing into processing limits perceptual exploration.

Several groups of young children (ten to twelve years old) were asked to consider the suggestion that 'bread, fish and milk should be made free for everyone'. Several of the children came from families so poor that they could not even afford to have milk every day. Yet none of the groups saw any great advantage in the idea. They were almost universally against the suggestion. How could this happen? It happened as a direct result of the perceptual narrowness that follows from the 'point-to-point' style of thinking that is so common with younger children. They declared that if these items were going to be free everyone would rush to the shops to get them. The shops would be crowded. The buses would be crowded. The drivers would go on strike. There would be chaos. That was one line of thought. Another line of thought started with everyone wanting the free food and then went on to the producers having trouble producing it, a disruption of the distribution system, since the shops would not make profits, and again a general breakdown of the system. Once a child had started along a line of thought he moved on from point to point. There was no attempt to direct attention in a broad perceptual sweep which might have shown up the advantages of the proposal.

A hungry man sits down at a table and a plate of chicken is placed in front of him. He is hungry so he eats it all up. But if his perception of the situation had been different his action would also have been different. If he had known that he had a long journey ahead of him with no prospect of further food he might have wrapped up some of the chicken and taken it with him. If he had known that his host was going to join him for the meal he might have waited for him to do so. If he had known that the chicken was possibly infected with salmonella he might have left it uneaten. If he had remembered that it was Friday and he did not eat meat on Friday he might have asked for something else. There is nothing complicated about any of these perceptions. They do not need working out. It is simply a matter of being aware of them. And that is one of the functions of thinking: to direct attention across the perceptual field.

We can look at three different situations in order to see the relationship between perception and processing.

In the first situation a couple are about to buy a house. They have to borrow some money by means of a mortgage. They are offered two choices. The ordinary mortgage spreads over twenty-five years at a rate of interest of 12 per cent. Capital has to be repaid throughout this period. The insurance-linked mortgage has an interest rate of 9 per cent but the insurance premiums have to be paid as well. There is no repayment of capital until the end, when it is paid from the insurance lump sum. This mortgage spreads over eighteen years. Which is the better mortgage? The couple would have to use mathematical processing to work out their payments per year (and per month). They would work out the total amount paid out in each case. They could make a decision based on the results of their mathematics. But there are other things which are not so easily fitted into this mathematical processing. What effect will inflation have on either scheme? What rate of inflation might be expected? What is the tax position on the mortgage interest? Will they be likely to move? What will happen to the insurance policy if they have to stop paying the premiums? What are their future earning prospects? A broad perceptual sweep is necessary if all these things are to be taken into account. In this example a combination of perceptual sweep and processing has to be used. Processing by itself is not enough.

A patient goes to see a doctor and complains that he has indigestion. The doctor asks where the pain is and the patient points towards his stomach. The doctor gives the patient some antacids, advises him about diet and asks him to come back in two weeks' time. He also tells him not to smoke or drink. A few hours later the patient collapses with a heart attack. Had the perceptual sweep of the doctor's been broader he might have asked when the pain had first occurred, whether it was related to food or exercise, how severe it was, whether there was pain down the left arm as well and many such questions. He might even have done an electrocardiograph, which might have shown cardiac ischaemia. He might still have been unable to detect the imminent heart attack (such is the nature of heart attacks), but he would have been more likely to make the correct diagnosis. Every patient would prefer his doctor to make as broad a perceptual sweep as possible to take in all the signs and symptoms and test results before arriving at his diagnosis. This example again involves a mixture of perception and processing. But here the emphasis is on perception. If the perceptual sweep is broad enough then the diagnosis is likely to suggest itself without too much further processing.

A man is offered a better job in a town some distance away. He can see at once that the pay is better. But taking up the job means selling his house and buying another. It means leaving the neighbourhood he knows and likes. It means leaving his friends and changing school for his children. He has to consider how his wife will feel about it. What sort of place is the new town? What are his prospects in his present job? What would his prospects be in the new job? Will the higher pay continue or will it be higher only at the beginning? What matters most to him in life? How important is the extra money? In this example the processing is relatively insignificant, but the perceptual sweep is crucial. His decision will be based on his values, his consideration of the factors involved, his understanding of the advantages and disadvantages and consequences, his consideration of the points of view of his wife and children and so on.

Information and perception

In each of the above examples it could be said that it was 'information' rather than 'perception' that mattered. It is very important to be quite clear about the distinction between information and perception. In education one is quite used to information being cut and dried and presented in textbooks or on data sheets. In such a case the function of perception is to direct attention to the information, to put different pieces of information together, to abstract certain things, to make predictions and so on.

In real-life situations outside school hours, information is never provided in such a neatly packaged form. Information is obtained by exploring experience, by asking questions, by knowing where to look for it and by making assumptions. To say that a person needs more information before he can start thinking is pointless, because thinking is concerned precisely with extracting that information from experience.

Perception is the processing of information for use. Thinking is the processing of information for use. We have defined thinking as the 'exploring of experience for a purpose'. That is why perception and thinking are the same thing.

Perceptual sweep

In this section much attention has been given to the idea of 'perceptual sweep' as a way of illustrating the role of perception in thinking. The deliberate directing of attention to as broad a field as possible is a very basic part of the skill of thinking. Nevertheless there are many other aspects of thinking skill. There are times when we must recognize certain patterns: different ways of being right; different ways of being wrong; types of evidence. At other times we may have to make judgements or decisions: about values; about belief and so on. Then certain operations have to be carried out: organizing; challenging concepts; asking questions. All these take place in the perception area. They are devices and frameworks for directing attention.

That perception can be improved by deliberate attention and practice may be seen in the results of an experiment in which two groups of children were asked to consider the proposal that all school-leavers should do a year's social service. One of the groups had done some of the thinking lessons and the other group had not. The trained group were able to consider many more aspects of the proposed situation. This was especially true of the practical points, which the untrained group tended to ignore.

Experiment

The pupils were grammar-school girls aged twelve or thirteen. One class of thirty-two pupils had done fourteen thinking lessons. The untrained class of sixteen pupils had not done any thinking lessons. Output took the form of an essay, with the research worker extracting ideas. In the table the points made by the untrained group have been doubled to make them comparable at a glance with the larger trained group.

Problem: 'What do you think of the idea that everyone should spend one year doing social service (e.g. helping old people, hospital work, cleaning up the environment etc.) after leaving school?'

	untrained group	trained group
points in favour of the idea	(90)	149
points against the idea	(98)	188
neutral, explanatory points	(82)	250
points affecting the pupil personally	(174)	224
points affecting other specific people	(28)	91
points relating to society as a whole	(16)	41
practical points about administration	(46)	209
TOTAL	(534)	1,152
average number of points per pupil	16·6	36

Patterns

'Patterns' is probably the most important word we have. Ever since Plato, the grand-daddy of western philosophers, concerned himself with form, all philosophers have been obsessed with the importance of pattern, form or idea. And so they should be. Pattern covers the areas of meaning, recognition and relationship. Pattern is the basis not only of how the mind works but of how the world itself works. Unfortunately pattern is so very important a word that its meaning is never very precisely defined and it can be applied to anything from organization to the decoration on wallpaper.

In previous sections we have seen that thinking is very largely to do with perception. In order to understand something of the process of the perception it is necessary to understand the nature of patterns. This section will attempt to show what patterns are, how they come to be formed and how they are used. The teaching method described later in the book is closely based on this understanding of patterns.

Because the word pattern means so many different things to different people, it is helpful to try to arrive at a usable definition that is simple and practical. On many occasions in the course of lectures I have asked members of the audience to write down a definition of 'pattern'. I have many hundreds of such cards from a wide variety of audiences. Some of the definitions are given below. They are not meant to be representative of the group from which they came.

Definitions of 'pattern'

From a group of teachers and educationalists:

'Repeating visual motif – formally arranged.'

'Shapes or designs which are repeated alternately or in sequence.'

'Series of shapes, lines arranged in a related way.'

'Repetition of forms in a non-random flow.'

'Repetition of motif, or function, related to rhythm.'

'Design which repeats and is pleasing to the eye.'

'A series of lines, shapes, colours or textures having some relation with each other.'

'Organized repetition of a motif.'

'A number of items arranged in a definite way.'

'Any shape or group of shapes which repeats or appears to repeat in a fairly regular manner.'

In these definitions there is a dominant theme of *repetition*. We also get concepts like: non-random, rhythm, relations, organized, arranged in a definite way. A repetition of a visual motif, as on wallpaper, is possibly the simplest form of organization or order. The motif is the same and the distance between motifs is the same.

From a group all of whom had an IQ in excess of 148:

'An arrangement of shapes in an artistic or regular form.'

'An ordered arrangement where each part is related to the other parts.'

'A structured form.'

'An ordered system of events.'

'An ordered array or arrangement of lines or events.'

'An associated group of anything that is not random.'

'Any display exhibiting regularity.'

'A regular arrangement of lines, dots and areas.'

'A group of things in which one thing has a direct relationship to another.'

'A systematic arrangement.'

These definitions are a little more general. The main theme is that of order. This is expressed as: structure, regular arrangement, systematic arrangement, direct relationship, non-random arrangement and so on.

From a group of computer people:

'A sequence of events or objects, certain aspects of which are related or repetitive.'

'Recognizable, or predictable series of events or objects.'

'A coordinated design.'

'A logical repetition of shapes or conditions.'

'A set of relationships of material or abstract things.'

The emphasis here is on relationships. We also see a hint of 'recognizable or predictable'.

From a group of philosophers:

'A pattern is that which some intelligent device (human, animal or machine) states to be a pattern.'

'An arrangement of phenomena that is meaningful to the percipient.'

'A pattern is something I can relate to previous knowledge.'

'Various characteristics, physical or mental, which can be recognized on different occasions.'

'A set of objects such that a human observing it sees a structure in addition to just the objects ... tautology? just using "structure" for pattern?'

In this group of definitions we see a marked shift from order and repetition within the *arrangement* itself to the importance of the *perceiving mind* which recognizes and relates to previous knowledge. It is fair to say that the controversy as to whether order exists in the arrangement or only in the mind of the observer has been just about the most permanent controversy in philosophy. Fortunately in our understanding of patterns we need not get involved in this highly artificial controversy.

What is a pattern?

I propose to use a very simple definition of a pattern and then show how this definition gives rise to the many aspects of it that are offered when people are asked to define a pattern. Instead of showing how these different aspects can be reduced to a fundamental principle I shall try to show how the principle can be built up into these aspects.

The definition: 'When the movement from the present state to the succeeding state occurs with a probability above chance then a pattern is present.'

This is illustrated in diagram 1. If the movement from A to B occurs with a probability above chance then there is a pattern. If the probability is very much greater than chance it is a strong pattern. If the probability is only just above chance it is a weak pattern.

The principle can be seen to apply to the repetition or rhythm aspect mentioned in so many definitions. In diagram 2 we see a repeating pattern. One of the circles is missing but we know what it should be and where it should be, so our placing of a new circle in that position is very much more than a chance happening. Similarly, if we are asked to extend a pattern we can do so quite easily since we know what to supply and where. So repetition gives us a right to expect something or to predict something. This links up with the predictability aspect of patterns which was also mentioned in the definitions.

Repetition is a special case of order. In fact it is probably the easiest form of order. Order implies that there is a reason for something being in some place. That reason may be spatial or mathematical or organizational. If we knew what the order was we could supply the missing item, if there was a missing item. Order gives us a means for predicting what comes next or what should be there. In diagram 3a we see a figure that looks like a square with a piece missing. Because we know the order involved in a square we can complete the square with a probability much higher than chance.

So far we have considered repetition, rhythm or order within the object that we have looked at. Of course there has to be an observer capable of noticing the order, but the order seems to lie in the situation. The order can, however, lie only in the observer. If a person knows that Jack and Jill are inseparable twins and he catches sight of Jack he will look around for Jill because he expects

Diagram 1

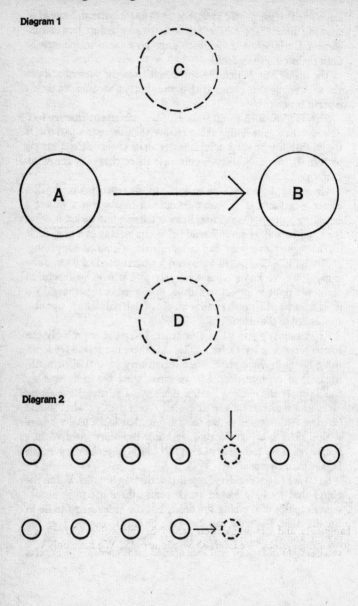

Diagram 2

to see Jill. In this case it is the observer's knowledge and experience which create the expectancy. Similarly in diagram 3b we can look at the arrangement of lines and move at once to the word 'square'. This is just as much moving along a pattern as is completing the square in diagram 3a. In both cases we are moving

Diagram 3

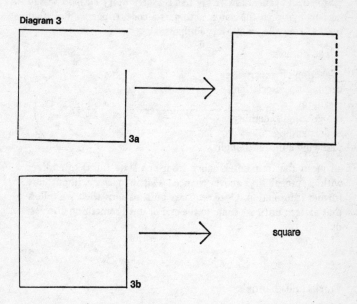

from one state to another with a probability greater than chance. Recognition is the use of patterns. We see something and we know what it is, what to call it and what to do with it, because we have experienced these associations in the past.

Codes

Languages and communication would be impossible without a patterning system. We establish words as codes. We have only to use a code for it to trigger off in the mind of the listener all the information we want him to have. The code acts as the beginning of a pattern and the mind moves along that pattern, turning up different associations. If we say the word 'school' to a child his mind moves along through all the associations of school: both personal and general. If we say to a teacher: 'Mary Philpott was in here today,' then the name, acting as a code, triggers off all that teacher's experience of Mary Philpott.

The phrases

triggering off experience
turning up associations
meaning
recognizing something
understanding
following a line of thought

all mean that our minds move from one state (idea) to another with a probability above chance. This happens without any further information. Once we start on a pattern then we follow that pattern until we come to the end or until something distracts us.

Tracks and channels

In diagram 4a we can see how in moving along a pattern we might move from A to B to E to F. We could just as easily represent all these different states as a road, channel or track, as shown in diagram 4b. The functional effect is the same. Once you are on a road you are more likely to proceed along the road than to jump over the hedge at the side. If we use this track notation we can also show the 'likelihood' or probability of our taking a certain road. We do this by altering the width of the road: a wide road is more likely to be followed than a narrow road. So in diagram 5 if we start at A we are more likely to end up at B than at C.

Diagram 4

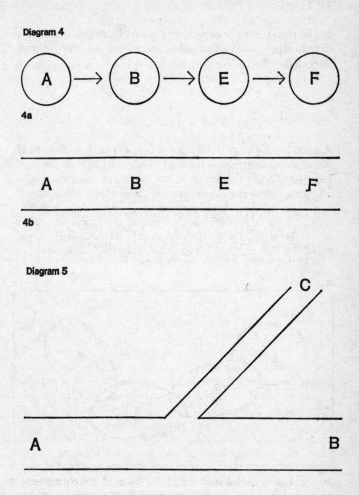

4a

4b

Diagram 5

Two information models

But how are the tracks or patterns formed? To understand this we
have to look at two information models that are very different
from each other.

The towel model

A towel is placed on a flat surface such as a table. A small bowl of
ink is placed alongside. A spoonful of ink is taken from the bowl
and poured on to the surface of the towel. An ink stain results.
The towel corresponds to the mind or the memory. It records and
keeps a record of all that happens to it. The ink stain corresponds
to the incoming information. We repeat the procedure with a
second, third and fourth spoonful of ink. At the end the towel
shows four ink stains as illustrated in diagram 6. The towel can

Diagram 6

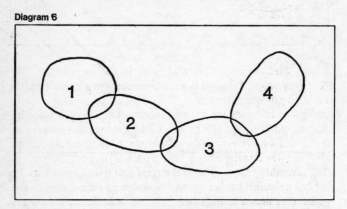

now be said to have a 'memory' of the things that have happened
to it (the ink input). The surface is neutral and passive. In order to
make use of the information stored on the surface we should have

to have some outside device which could be brought to the surface and which would count or measure the ink stains.

The jelly model

The jelly or gelatine model replaces the towel with a large shallow dish of gelatine that has set. The bowl of ink is now heated up. When a spoonful of hot ink is poured on to the gelatine surface the hot ink starts to dissolve the gelatine. But the ink cools down and stops dissolving the gelatine. When the ink and melted gelatine are mopped up or poured off, a shallow depression is left in the surface of the gelatine. This 'imprint', or effect on the surface, corresponds to the ink stain on the towel surface. We now pour a

Diagram 7

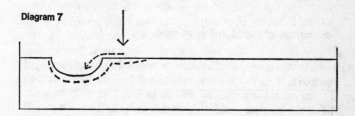

second, third and fourth spoonful on to the surface in exactly the same way as we did with the towel model. But this time something very different happens.

The hot ink from the second spoonful tends to flow into the depression left by the first spoonful. This depression is made even deeper and a relatively shallow depression is left where the second spoonful was actually placed. This process is shown in diagram 7. The same thing happens with the third and fourth spoonfuls. In the end a channel has been eroded or sculpted in the surface of the gelatine, as shown in diagram 8.

Diagram 8

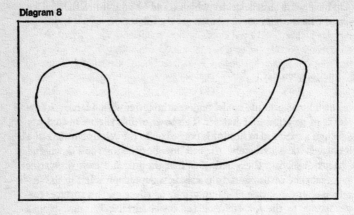

Comparison of towel and jelly models

In the towel model the information is recorded separately and kept separately. If we call the first ink stain G and the fourth K then the two remain separate and we can look at G or K as we wish. But in the gelatine model a channel is formed. If we put in a K spoonful it will not remain as K but will wander along the channel to end up just as though we had put in a G spoonful. So the surface has *created* a channel or pattern whereby it moves from a K to a G input. As soon as the surface receives a K input it reacts just as though it has received a G input. No outside processor is necessary. The recording surface has created its own way of organizing information.

Relevance to the mind and perception

The mind is not a shallow dish of gelatine. The relevance of the jelly model to the physiological and functional behaviour of the mind is described in detail in my book *The Mechanism of Mind*. In that book we can see how the nerves, synapses and feedback system give a functional organization related to the jelly model. In effect what we have in the jelly model is a system that *allows incoming information to arrange itself into patterns*. In other words a self-educating system. Self-educating systems are pattern creating and pattern-using systems. The patterns are created from the *sequence* of the incoming information. The first piece of information alters the state of the mind so that the second piece becomes associated with it or linked to it. In this way patterns are built up.

All the psychological and physiological evidence that we have suggests that with regard to perception the human mind is a pattern-making and pattern-using system.

The behaviour of patterns

Having looked at the nature of patterns and the formation of patterns or tracks we can now look at *some* of the phenomena that arise in a patterning system.

Humour

Humour can happen only in a patterning system. Diagram 9 shows how a person starting at A will move to B because the track is wider. The track to C is present but is ignored. If, however, attention is drawn directly to C then with *hindsight* it becomes obvious that C could have been reached from A.

As a basic example of humour we can look at a child's riddle: 'What is yellow and white and goes at five hundred miles per hour.' We tend to think of some painted aeroplane as we move down the track from A to B. But the answer is: 'A jumbo-jet pilot's egg sandwich.' This takes us to the point C. With hindsight it is obvious. We had been looking for something that was yellow and white and flew by itself rather than something that was *carried* in a flying device.

The millionaire was complaining that he had had a very bad Christmas because he had been given only three golf clubs. And what is more only two of them had swimming pools! This is the standard pun. The usual meaning of 'golf club' takes one down the A to B track. The less usual meaning puts us at C and with hindsight this is seen to be just plausible.

Diagram 9

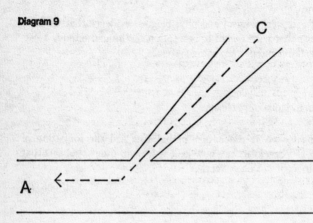

This basic process is repeated in all humour situations. Sometimes no dominant track is indicated but instead the listener is given A and then given C and asked to imagine how they might be connected. Finally a very obscure, but just plausible, connection between C and A is revealed. There are many variations on the use of the basic process and much of the power of humour arises from social expectations, prejudices, emotions, malice and so on, quite apart from the basic mechanics.

Insight

Insight involves exactly the same process as humour, except that in the case of humour the end result is only just plausible whereas in that of insight it is more effective than the starting idea.

A tennis tournament is run on the usual elimination basis. Two players play each other and the winner plays the winner of another match. A number of rounds are played until the players are sufficiently reduced in number for there to be semi-finals and then a final match. On this occasion in the singles section there are 131 entrants. The problem is to find the smallest number of matches that would have to be played to provide a winner.

There are a number of ways of solving this problem. Most of them involve pencil and paper and finding out how many byes there would be in the first round. This is the A to B approach given in diagram 9. If, however, instead of being interested in the winner, we shift our attention to the losers, we find that there must be 130 losers, since there can be only one winner in a singles tennis tournament. As there has to be one game for each loser (neither more nor less) the smallest number of matches must be 130. It is as simple as that and so simple that many people get quite upset. In the diagram we are now at point C and with *hindsight* the route from A is obvious.

Asymmetry

This very basic property of patterning systems is implicit in humour and insight and in the 'glide-past' effects to be considered shortly. What it means is that in a patterning system the path from one point to another is usually very different from the path from the second point back to the first. In other words the path from to X to Y is different from the path from Y to X. We can call this asymmetry.

If you give people the words 'dog' and 'knife' and ask them to give the next association you get a very different result from what would happen if you give them 'knife' and then 'dog'. I have done

Diagram 10

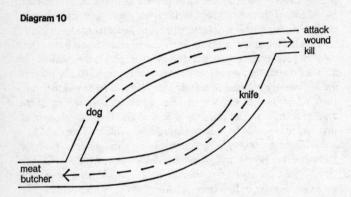

this experiment on a number of occasions in the course of my lectures. In the dog–knife sequence the concepts of 'kill, wound, attack' occur *five times* as often as in the knife–dog sequence. Conversely the concepts of 'meat, butcher, food' occur almost twice as often in the knife–dog sequence as in the dog–knife sequence.

An explanation of this is shown in diagram 10. It may be seen that on starting from KNIFE the domestic use of a knife is a stronger track than the criminal use and so the 'eating' track of a dog links in. If we start from DOG, however, the 'vicious' track seems stronger than the 'eating' track and this leads to the criminal use of a knife.

In other experiments people were asked to connect up the two words 'telephone' and 'cow'. Those asked to connect 'telephone' to 'cow' made various connections via ring-bull-cow, bell-cow, Alexander Graham Bell-bell-cow, or even the shape of a telephone and the shape of a cow's horns. In the reverse direction the route was quite different, usually involving some story in which the cow was ill and the vet had to be telephoned or the cow had wandered out of a field and the farmer had to be telephoned. Diagram 11 illustrates this effect.

Diagram 11

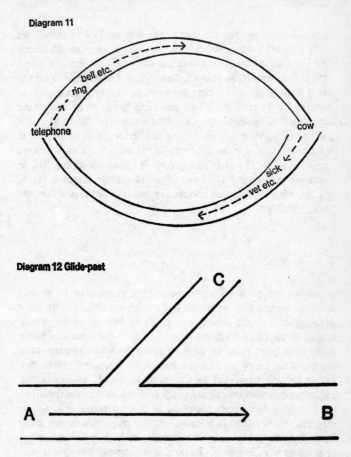

Diagram 12 Glide-past

Glide-past

Quite often in our thinking, or in the way we look at things, we glide past an alternative because the main track is so dominant. We know about this alternative and can easily see it if our attention is drawn to it. So smooth, however, is the passage down the main track (diagram 12) that our attention never has a chance to move along the track to C. To combat this glide-past effect we need some method of holding our attention at the junction: some method of making us pause. This deliberate pause allows us at least to acknowledge the existence of the other track and then we can consider it. The glide-past process is fundamental and will be discussed in greater detail later. Many of the operations in teaching thinking are designed specifically to carry out this 'deliberate pause' function.

Point-to-point

If we set out to think about something there may be several different aspects that we ought to consider: several different lines of thought, as shown in diagram 13. We do, however, have to take one of these. Once we have started along a track we can move along from point to point. Each point we reach becomes the starting point for a new track. Sometimes, with younger children, the points become irrelevant to the main theme. With others the points remain relevant but are much less important than the other tracks which have been neglected at the beginning (C1, C2 in diagram 13). We tend to follow along the track. We do not automatically have a mechanism for bringing us back to the beginning to consider parallel tracks. To do this we have to have some outside framework. Part of the aim of teaching thinking is to provide such a framework, for without it the mind does not naturally abandon one track to take up another.

Diagram 13   Point-to-point

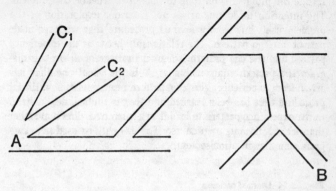

Artificial framework

The patterns or tracks in our minds are built up by our experience. We explore our experience by moving along the paths of
association and knowledge. But we can also set up artificial patterns. There is no natural reason, for example, why a search for
'plus' points should be followed by a search for 'minus' points and
then by a search for 'interesting' points. This sequence occurs only
if we have artificially decided that it should. The natural sequence
would be to consider the situation, move into a judgement and
then follow up the judgement.

Parallel patterns

In practice it is only in daydreams that we follow just one pattern.
Usually we have at least two patterns. The first is the experience
pattern, which consists of our experience and knowledge tracks
and associations. The second is our ego pattern, which deals with
what we are trying to do. We oscillate between the two. For in-

stance in solving a problem the ego pattern might compel us to restate the problem from time to time or to redefine the problem. The intention to do this arises not from our exploration of the problem itself but from a learned procedure that we have made part of our ego pattern. The relationship between the experience pattern and the ego pattern is shown in diagram 14. In this diagram the pattern commencing at A is the usual one that has arisen from experience. The 'ego' pattern represents some artificial procedure that has been learned and that is applied, deliberately, to the experience pattern to lead it in a 'preferred' direction rather than let it follow its own course. The ego pattern used here suggests some classification system.

Diagram 14 Learned patterns

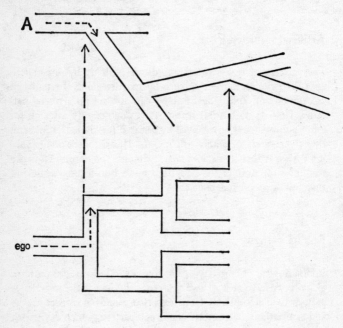

Teaching thinking

The mind is full of the patterns created by experience and knowledge. In order to make the best use of them we cannot simply drift along them from one point to another. In order to direct attention, or to hold it in areas it might otherwise have glided past, we need to create some artificial frameworks that we can use deliberately.

Patterns and errors

In the patterning world of perception, 'errors' are quite different from the errors we find in logic or in mathematics. It is no longer a matter of truth or falsity but of a sort of drift along one pattern and away from another. The preceding section examined the nature and formation of patterns. Against this background we can now look at some of the 'errors' that can arise in a patterning system. The subject matter for this examination will be the notion of teaching thinking as a skill.

Capture

Capture occurs when one channel has been very well established and the alternative channel much less clearly defined. The process is illustrated in diagram 15. When one sets out to teach thinking as a skill one finds that the 'logic' concept has been so long established that it is at once assumed that one is trying to teach logic. It is then claimed that this is nothing new and that it has often been done. It is also claimed that teaching logic does not have much relevance to the practical use of thinking in everyday life. It is very difficult to indicate that one is not setting out to teach logic but wishes to establish another channel called 'perception'. In some cases the two channels do not even exist, since the term 'logic' has been expanded to include anything that is to do with thinking and is correct and useful. This is a dangerous situation because the meaning of the term 'logic' has come to embrace all of thinking, but the actual process remains confined to the rules of formal logic. This extreme type of 'capture' occurs with many other long-established concepts.

Diagram 15 Capture effect

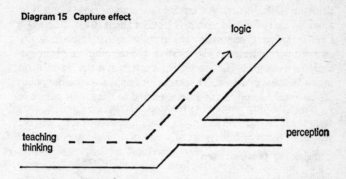

Because I originated the term 'lateral thinking', and because my name has been associated with it, another type of 'capture' occurs. When I talk about the teaching of thinking as a skill in schools it is at once assumed that I am referring to lateral thinking. Often a lecture or talk is labelled in this manner. Yet only one of the six sections in my own thinking programme is about lateral thinking. The other sections deal with the ordinary routine processes of thinking without any special creative element. But since the lateral-thinking channel has been well established it is difficult to show that the programme as a whole is quite different.

Glide-past

In 'capture' we can see the path we want to take but are prevented from taking it because we are diverted along the established path. In the 'glide-past' effect we are prevented from even seeing the alternative path because we glide along the established path. In the first case we are diverted away from where we want to go. In the second case we are unable to see the diversion. So in capture the diversion is used against us, whereas in glide-past we would like to use the diversion but cannot do so.

In teaching thinking one has to have some content, since abstract philosophizing makes little impact. The content is used as illustrative example and also as a means for practising the various thinking skills. But content tends to have much more moment-to-moment carry-forward. At any one moment there is enough interest to carry one on to the next moment. Interesting discussions get under way: about crime, about pollution, about personal relationships. The process is forgotten and the lesson turns into a 'discussion' lesson. The teacher is happy because the pupils are obviously involved and interested and so they must surely be

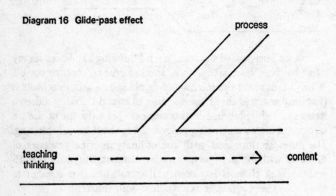

Diagram 16 Glide-past effect

learning something. The pupils themselves are far more interested in pursuing the content than in being dragged back to the thinking process involved. As a result, little attention is paid to the process and no transferable skill in thinking is developed. This glide-past effect is illustrated in diagram 16. In order to keep attention firmly on the process it is necessary to have a tight structure with a given time limit. If a variety of different problems is tackled for only a short length of time this prevents the glide effect from developing and makes it easier to look at the process involved in each of the problems.

Polarization

Quite often polarization is used deliberately in order to counter the capture effect. I am well aware that in this book, as indeed in some other books of mine, I am guilty of creating an exaggerated polarization between logic and perception. In practice the two are much closer and they tend to overlap and intermingle. But in order to avoid the capture effect; 'Oh you are talking about logic and we know all about logic', it is necessary to emphasize the differences and contrasts. The polarization effect is illustrated in diagram 17. Logic and perception are seen as part of thinking. They are closely connected. But it is possible to concentrate on the differences and to follow the ever-widening polarization paths to

Diagram 17 Polarization effect

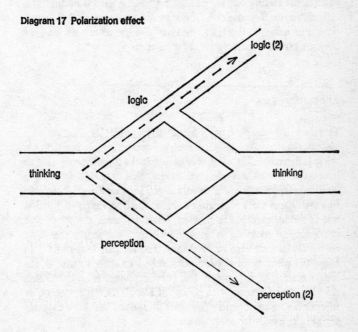

logic (2)

logic

thinking

thinking

perception

perception (2)

reach the points marked logic (2) and perception (2), which are strongly polarized positions.

The same polarization effect occurs with 'feeling' and 'thinking'. Some people protest that thinking is abstract and cold and that human feeling is all that matters. It is not easy to maintain that both feeling and thinking are required: that thinking without feeling is irrelevant and that feeling without thinking is limited and dangerous.

A polarization is quickly developed to show that feeling and thinking are two distinct things and that thinking is definitely anti-feeling. Thereafter any attempt to teach thinking as a skill is seen to be an attack on the importance of feeling.

In a patterning system it is really very difficult to maintain a balanced position. It is difficult to say that one is not against logic but against the exclusivity of logic. It is difficult to say that one is not against feeling but for combining feeling with thinking. The difficulty arises because one cannot straddle two tracks at the same time. Furthermore the tracks tend to diverge more and more as they are pursued, deliberately, to their ends.

The hump effect

This is a most important, difficult and dangerous effect in any biological system. A biological system operates by moving towards what is desirable. But what is desirable at the moment may lead to long-term harm. Conversely something that is good in the long term may require immediate sacrifice. The schoolboy who wants to leave school early is moving towards the desirability of earning and spending money. His parents, however, want him to go over the 'hump' of studying in order to be better qualified, so that later on in life he may earn more money. The fat person may have to forgo the pleasure of the immediate meal in order to slim in the longer term. The expression 'hump effect' comes from the notion that it may be necessary to go uphill initially, even if one's true intention is to coast gently downhill thereafter. You have to go up the ski slope in order to ski down.

The hump effect may also involve going in the opposite direction in order to go in the right direction eventually. A chicken is separated from some food by a wire fence. The chicken looks directly at the food and tries to get through the fence. The chicken remains on the same spot trying to get the food. In the same situation a dog will *move* away from the food and try to find his way round the fence. The dog is prepared to go in a different direction in order to achieve his aim. The chicken insists on getting there directly – and fails.

In teaching thinking, as in teaching other subjects, it may sometimes be necessary to label something which everyone knows with a label which no one knows. This is done on purpose in order to make something that would otherwise be taken for granted strange enough to get the attention it deserves. At first sight the labels will appear as unnecessary jargon and will be condemned as such, because a straightforward discussion without labels seems more attractive. But, as in the case of the chicken, one may have to go away from the obvious and along the less attractive path in order to reach the desired destination.

Diagram 18 illustrates the hump effect in that the most obvious and attractive path tends to be taken. Yet, to get the effect one wants, it may be necessary to pass along the unobvious and difficult path.

Diagram 18 Hump effect

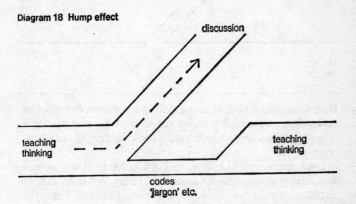

The sufficiency effect

The sufficiency effect has been mentioned at various points in the preceding sections. It is a sort of 'magnitude error'. In the magnitude error it is claimed that something will affect something else. Logically this is true, but in practice the magnitudes are such that the effect will not happen. For instance economic sanctions will cause a country to surrender: in practice the magnitude of the effect is quite insufficient. It is claimed that 'thinking' has always been taught in every subject and that therefore no new attempt need be made to teach thinking directly as a skill. Manifestly it is true that thinking is taught in every subject. But is this sufficient?

Diagram 19 Sufficiency effect

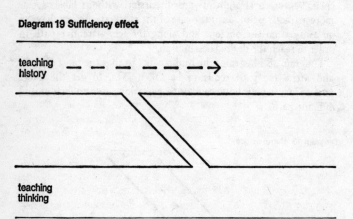

How much transferable thinking skill does one learn in history or geography or French? Remember the story of the man who said that he did not need to buy any more books because he had one at home.

The sufficiency effect is illustrated in diagram 19. It may be seen that there is a track from the teaching of history to the teaching of thinking. In practice this track is far less likely to be used than the content track. But logically it is there. And if one wishes to focus attention on it and to demonstrate how it exists then it is always possible to do so.

Complacency is often regarded as being synonymous with the sufficiency effect, but complacency may be a defence against doing anything further, whereas the sufficiency effect can be a genuine failure to appreciate that what is there in logical terms may not be there in practical terms. Logically you can show that there is a route from the market in a town to the railway station that takes only five minutes. But if no one knows the route and no one uses the route there is obviously a difference between theory and practice.

The sufficiency effect arises when attention is deliberately paid to a path, thereby raising its dominance temporarily with the intention of demonstrating that the dominance is in fact present in the system.

The peripheralism effect

This effect is especially important in the teaching of thinking. The mind likes to have something it can tackle and about which it can make definite judgements. Our scholastic tradition quite rightly emphasizes depth and accuracy in our work. The result is that our minds tend to move along the tracks that exist and to pursue a track as far as it will go rather than break off to follow something vague. The effect is seen most markedly in science. There are areas of science where we have analytical tools and also experimental systems. People work in these areas and are carried along on the momentum of their research to produce excellent papers on subjects that can best be described as 'peripheral'. Areas that are much larger and much more important are neglected because there is no easy way of tackling them. These more important areas are amorphous and subjective and it is difficult to apply the rigours of scientific method to them. So instead of wallowing around in these important areas and ending up with no results the scientist prefers to exercise his skill and achieve his reputation in a peripheral area which allows him to come up with something definite. Scholarship is too often the triumph of form over content.

Diagram 20 Peripheralism effect

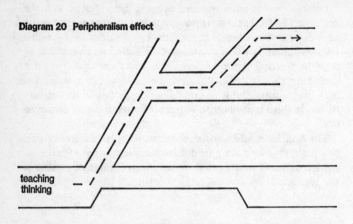

The peripheralism effect is illustrated in diagram 20. The mind moves along the broad path rather than into the indefinite path. It moves forward. It moves down a peripheral branch and then down another branch. In the end it may be quite far away from the area of importance, but so long as there is somewhere to move ahead of it, it moves forward. It is difficult to break off and to look at things in a broad fashion. Scholars spend their lives studying one period in the life of a poet who lived in the sixteenth century. It is there to be studied. There is enough detail. It is more secure than studying the poetic inclinations of schoolchildren (how do you study them?). Similarly in our approach to thinking we spend a great deal of time studying quite exotic and peripheral mathematical processes simply because they are there to be studied and can be demonstrated in an interesting fashion. They may be of no use at all to most of the pupils. Yet the broad areas of thinking, such as making decisions, are neglected because they are less tangible.

Approaches
to the teaching of thinking

'You cannot teach people to think – only things about which to think.'

This remark made by a teacher in a discussion on the teaching of thinking as a skill sums up the attitude of the majority of people. Thinking is seen to be the natural exercise of innate intelligence. Increased effectiveness in thinking is to come from increased knowledge and a greater fluency. In spite of this attitude there have been various approaches to the teaching of thinking. Some of these approaches are discussed in this section.

Formal logic

This is perhaps the most distinct attempt to teach thinking as a deliberate skill. Logic has had a place on the timetable of several schools and there are examinations in the subject. Logic is a subject that is definite and tangible. It involves principles and axioms. It satisfies the desire of those who regard ordinary thinking only as an imperfect form of mathematics and who desire to formalize thinking until it can have the precision of mathematics. There have been different approaches to the teaching of logic. The basic Aristotle/Aquinas approach was centred on the syllogism and the rules of syllogisms. Venn diagrams reinforced this approach. Lately this basis has been extended to include other elements of logic. Then there is the more mathematical approach which can include mathematical logic itself. More recently there is the approach based on computer logic.

It must be admitted that logic is a good way of teaching logic. It must also be admitted that most of the developments in the teaching of logic have been internal developments arising from the subject itself, and not from considerations of its practical applicability as a thinking tool. As has been discussed at various points in this book, logic is only part of thinking. The direct use of the deductive process forms only a very small part of ordinary thinking. The emphasis upon it in education arises from the type of artificial problem that is so often used. In such problems all the information is given and some basic principles can be applied. In real life, information is very rarely complete and there may be no basic principles at all. The main deficiency of logic is the starting point. Where does one start? Logic works to make clear what is implicit in the starting premises. But those are a matter of perceptual choice and patterning. Correctly applied logic can come to a contradictory conclusion if the starting point is altered.

The rules of logic do matter, but unfortunately the perfection of the subject does not guarantee its usefulness as a practical way of teaching thinking.

By-product of the teaching of other subjects

'If a person is thinking about something then surely he is learning how to think.'

Unfortunately this is not true. A geography teacher would claim that in learning geography a pupil would be forced to think. A history teacher and a science teacher would make the same claim. All would be right. The question is whether thinking about something develops any transferable skill in thinking. In 'content' subjects, the momentum of the subject is usually such that little attention can be paid to the actual process. Exhortations to 'think about it' or to consider 'what these things imply' merely ask the pupil to delve more deeply into his knowledge and find the right answer. In a content subject you cannot really think ahead of the content, because your speculation must always be very inferior to the actual facts. There is comparatively little scope for thinking except of the hindsight variety: 'Now you can see that this happened because of that and that . . .' When teachers appear to lead the thinking of their pupils towards a new insight the pupils' responses are usually so tightly shaped that it is more a matter of guessing what the teacher wants said next than of thinking the matter through. This is no fault of the teacher. It is the nature of content subjects that is at fault. Content is much more interesting than the thinking process. A pupil knows that with a little knowledge and a lot of thinking he will not do as well as the pupil who has a lot of knowledge and only a little thinking.

The other limitation of content subjects as a method of teaching thinking is that the thinking skills, even if they are learned, are rather limited. Classification, chains of explanation, the putting together of facts to reach a conclusion are all important in thinking, but they are only a small part of the total skill of thinking, which includes such things as decision, priorities, other people's views, problem-solving, conflict, guessing, emotional bias, prejudice and so on. We cannot pretend that situations consist only of pure information and the way it is handled in the mind.

It is probably true that a teacher who had a definite process framework could use a content subject for the teaching of thinking. But he would have to make a deliberate effort to focus attention on the processes. It would be futile to hope that adequate discussion of the content would eventually crytallize itself into transferable thinking skills.

Special subject teaching

It was often claimed that the justification for teaching Latin as a subject was that it trained the mind and developed thinking skill. It could be argued that if content subjects failed to teach thinking because the importance of the content obscured the thinking process, then a subject in which the content was irrelevant would teach thinking because attention could be focused only on the process. But although the subject might be irrelevant, it was the complex rules of the subject that determined the correctness of an answer, not the amount of thinking involved. Once again knowledge was more important than thinking.

The problem of transfer is always present. As a demonstration of deductive thinking Euclidean geometry is superb. A few axioms are built into theorems. The theorems are then applied to solve problems. I doubt if there has ever been a philosopher or a teacher who has not wished for a thinking system as controlled and as perfect. But, alas, excellence at geometry is of little help in solving problems outside architecture and engineering.

Debate and discussion

Unlike content subjects, debate and discussion do not rely on the manipulation of a knowledge reservoir. The thinking involved is more important than recourse to its basis in knowledge. For this reason it is sometimes felt that they provide a good training ground for thinking. The difficulty is that both debate and discussion are concerned with making and defending a case. This adversary type of thinking is undoubtedly useful in adversary situations such as the law or politics, but it is positively dangerous in almost all other situations. The defence of a position can involve excellent logic and ingenuity but it can also involve the most deliberate perceptual blindness. The scoring of debating points might be a debating triumph, but it does little to help with the genuine exploration of the subject. As was indicated earlier in this book, proving the other fellow wrong does not prove you right. Articulateness, fluency, confidence and quick thinking may all be improved by debate and discussion. All of these qualities frequently masquerade most successfully as thinking skill. And yet if one compares the thinking content of a discussion among articulate pupils with the thinking content of a discussion among less articulate pupils there is no difference. At first sight the fluency of expression is misleading.

Discussion is certainly a good practice ground for thinking, but by itself it is insufficient because it does not develop any transferable skill other than a critical skill in spotting weaknesses in an argument. Useful as it may be, critical skill is quite insufficient as a total thinking skill, even though education has always placed so much emphasis on it.

Games, puzzles and simulations

Since the 'process' of games is so much more important than the 'content' it is felt that the practice of game skills should develop thinking skills. It is quite true that games situations offer an opportunity to practise a very much wider range of skills than do content subjects. In a game something is happening all the time. Your thinking can bring about a situation or avoid a situation. Such things as strategy, planning and decision are an integral part of most games. Once you know the rules of the game knowledge is very much less important than thinking skill. All these things should make the games situation an ideal one for developing thinking skills.

Yet paradoxically it is the very excellence of the game situation which limits its use for training thinking. The problem is one of transfer. It is difficult to transfer skills that are learned in a specific game to more general situations. Ideally a game would have to be so close to real life as to be indistinguishable from it in order to develop the appropriate skills. Games have an internal logic and a good player quickly learns this internal logic because it is repeated so often. Life, unfortunately, has no such internal logic and each situation requires some basic thinking skills rather than knowledge of the supposed internal logic.

Games are useful for generating attitudes and insights into one's own thinking processes. A game situation can quickly show up a habit of mind. Games provide useful windows into thinking and behaviour. But the thinking skills involved are so specialized that they are difficult to transfer.

Philosophy

The teaching of philosophy and the history of ideas teaches how men's minds have worked and may extract some basic principles of thinking. But a passive description of thinking does little to develop an active skill. The fact that subjects such as philosophy are 'about' thinking does not mean that they teach thinking.

Psychology

The philosopher is concerned with the result of his thinking skills, whereas the psychologist is concerned with the nature of the skills themselves. Psychologists are good at description. The thinking process may be divided up into observation, analysis, abstraction, model-making, expectancy, motivation and so on. This may be a useful description. But you cannot simply take the parts of a description and turn them into tools. You cannot say 'observation' is part of thinking, so we ought to practise observation. You cannot say that because motivation is also part of thinking we ought to practise 'motivating'. There is a big difference between a tool and an element of description. If you wanted someone to start a motor-car you could give him an explanation of what happens in an internal combustion engine or you could give him explicit instructions about using the ignition key. An operating tool in thinking may be quite different from a psychological description of the thinking process. For instance 'intuition' is a useful psychological description but impossible to use as an operating tool. On the other hand an artificial device like the word 'po' has no psychological meaning but can be a practical operating tool.

Various attempts have been made to teach thinking based on the division of the process into its component psychological parts. These are based on the misconception that if you turn a descriptive element back to front it becomes a tool. It does not. Nor does understanding of a process provide a means for using that process.

Rules, use, skill and tools

Learning the rules of thinking does not develop a practical skill in thinking. Using thinking in particular situations develops thinking skill in those situations, but not a transferable skill in thinking. Skill has to be person-centred, not situation-centred. The dilemma is that it is usually possible to teach only situation-centred skills. You train a person to behave in a certain way in a certain situation. The way out of the dilemma is to create situations that are *themselves* transferable. We call such situations *tools*. A person is trained in the tool situation. He learns how to cope with the tool. The tool and his skill in using it can now be transferred to new situations. It does not in the least matter whether the tool is strictly necessary or not. An unnecessary tool can still act as a transfer device.

Part Two

Introduction to Part Two

The first part of this book was concerned with the background to the teaching of thinking, general concepts and observations and a theoretical framework. No doubt there are other theoretical frameworks which are as plausible and which will have their adherents, but since this book is intended to be practical it has not been my intention to ride more than one horse at a time. Had I done so the result would have been a review of various approaches – and a very different book.

The theoretical framework and concepts introduced in the first part to the book have, in practice, been incorporated into an actual thinking programme which endeavours to treat thinking as a skill in the school curriculum. This programme is now in use, in one way or another, in about 20 per cent of secondary schools in Britain and in many schools overseas – even as far afield as Papua New Guinea. Some schools are using the programme in a thorough way and teaching the new subject to all classes, right across the school, at a certain age level. Others are trying it out as a special subject with one particular class. Some schools use it in the English department. Others treat it as part of general studies or as a core subject to such amorphous subjects as integrated studies or interdisciplinary inquiry. In many cases the head himself teaches thinking as his 'contact lesson'. In other cases the schools are still studying the material for future use or reference.

The programme is called 'CoRT Thinking'. The name derives from the initials of the Cognitive Research Trust, with the extra vowel introduced to make it pronounceable as a word. Many schools simply refer to the subject as 'Cort' and so avoid the awkward self-consciousness of teaching 'thinking'. The programme

consists of six sections, each of which has ten lessons and covers a
general theme such as breadth, organization, interaction, creativity, information and feeling, and action. Each lesson focuses on a
single attention area, for example 'guessing' or 'decision' or
'Defining the Problem'. In some cases the thinking operation
round which the lesson centres is crystallized into a specific 'tool'.
For example the very first lesson, which involves looking at the
plus, minus and interesting points in a situation – instead of
reaching an initial judgement – is called PMI and the children
are taught to 'do a PMI'. There are a number of these crystallized
tools, but most lessons focus on a single area in order to give
pupils some insight into that process and some practice in that
area, for example 'conclusion' or 'evaluation'. For each lesson
every pupil has a coloured leaflet which both explains the point of
the lesson and gives the practice items. The cover of the leaflet
usually illustrates in visual form the process of the lesson.

In the lessons the children work in groups. The teacher introduces the point of the lesson, preferably by way of a topical
example, and then the groups use that thinking process on a variety of problems. The emphasis is on having a number of different
practice problems so that attention remains focused on the process
rather than on the content.

Each of the six sections has a teacher's handbook which gives
the background to that section, comments on the teaching of
thinking as a subject and specific teachers' notes for each of the
ten lessons in that section. It has not been possible to organize
teacher training, but the majority of teachers have been able to
introduce the material without any special training. There is a
certain amount of awkwardness the first time but confidence
grows with use. Some teachers might of course have benefited
greatly from training and may drop out in its absence.

The programme has been used across a very wide range of ages
and abilities. In general the age range is from nine-year-olds at
primary school to sixteen-year-olds at secondary school. At the
extremes the material has been taught to five-year-olds in the Unitarian Church Sunday schools and to IBM executives at the
company's European headquarters. This is possible only because
individual teachers have been able to adapt the basic framework to

fit the needs of their own particular class. Working within the general framework, teachers select the practice problems or invent their own. They also adapt the concepts to suit their pupils' understanding. On the ability side the spread has been just as great. The programme has been taught to pupils with IQs ranging from 83 (almost ESN) to 140. One youngster with an IQ of around 80 made the following comment at the end of the PMI lesson: 'And if you buy a television, and say to yourself, "Oh I want that television", but when you've bought it, then you think how much it's going to cost you, you'd wish you hadn't bought it. But if you'd done a PMI first you'd be better.'

The second part of this book deals with the practical operation of this thinking programme. Some of the points that arise may be specific to this particular programme. Others would apply to any attempt to teach thinking as a skill. There are also points that apply to any curriculum innovation, whether it has to do with thinking or not. The quotations used here are not intended to be testimonials. They are the candid comments of teachers who are teaching thinking in this manner. They are quoted anonymously because there was no original intention to publish them – and in some cases the teacher may have changed his mind. If they seem positive that is because the teachers using the material are usually motivated to do so. Teachers who dislike the approach would probably not become involved in using it. Quite the most striking aspect of the feedback from teachers has been its extraordinary variability. One teacher may condemn an aspect of the programme that is highly praised by another. Views are quite often completely contradictory. For example, the practice item which asked children to consider whether all cars should be painted yellow was often singled out as an instance of a problem that was abstract, irrelevant and even frivolous by some teachers, and yet other teachers quoted it as an example of an item that children of all ability levels could tackle. The contradictions seem to be explained by different expectations, different preconceptions, different teaching styles and different classroom circumstances. In a field as personal as thinking these differences are accentuated.

This part of the book is not meant to be an *analysis* of the CoRT project. It is too early for that. Since teaching is as much a practical subject as a theoretical one, this second part of the book is about the practical teaching of thinking. Discussion about the practical teaching of thinking must be based on some *actual* teaching of thinking. The CoRT programme simply provides the actual teaching of thinking on which the observations can be based.

We can start by considering some of the basic tools used in a practical approach to the teaching of thinking.

Tools for teaching thinking

Different strategies can be used for finding one's way round an unknown town. Each of the strategies has specific advantages (reliability, speed of learning and so on) and disadvantages (incompleteness, lack of transfer and so on). The strategies can be summarized under a number of heads.

The knowledge approach

You might study the town systematically in the way that learner-taxidrivers drive around on mopeds studying the town before taking their 'knowledge test'. You might choose to study one area thoroughly and then move on to an adjoining area. Or you might choose to study the whole town in a hierarchical fashion by learning first the major routes and then the lesser roads and so on down to the back alleys. You might study the town by poring over maps and setting yourself tests, or by actually moving about the streets and trying to find your way from one area to another. You might prefer to make no systematic study at all but just to live in the town and wait for your familiarity with it to grow with use. It is true that with this last approach there might remain areas of the town that you never get to know because you have never visited them, but you might feel that this does not matter since your knowledge should match only the use you intend to make of it.

The formula approach

This could also be called the 'specific operations' approach. In contrast to the knowledge approach it is extremely rapid and reliable. You make no attempt to get to know the streets and districts of the town. Instead you devise or use certain 'formulae' that are based on the town's transport system.

'Take a number 19 bus and get off opposite the big red store.'

'Take a Piccadilly Line underground train to Leicester Square then change to the Northern Line. Get off at the third stop.'

With such formulae you can quickly establish efficient routes and get to know the parts of the town you are going to use. The areas in between will remain totally unknown, but this may not matter to you. All you have to remember to do is to get on at the right station, let the system carry you along its predictable route and get off at the right station. In other words you plug in the appropriate formula, follow it along, then look at the results. This is a bit like studying for exams. You learn lists and model answers. If you are asked the sort of question you expect then you plug in the appropriate list and write it down. It is also like using cookbook formulae or logarithms.

The general operations approach

The knowledge approach is thorough but it takes a great deal of time and effort. Furthermore until the knowledge is considerable it is very difficult to use any of it. Unless the town is very interesting it is also difficult to be enthusiastic about learning your way round street by street. You may also have to accumulate far more knowledge than you really need for your own living purposes. Finally the knowledge method has no transfer at all to a new town. No matter how thoroughly you get to know the old town this will not help you when you move to a new town.

The formula approach is fast and reliable. But there may be no easy formulae or transport system for reaching some places. You tend to be restricted to those places for which formulae can be found. You are the slave of available formulae. You cannot transfer to a new town the specific formulae that have been developed for a particular town.

The 'general operations' method is less exact and less reliable than either of the other two methods. But it is simple to learn and can be transferred to any new town. The method consists of developing some general operations, such as: learning how to ask the way; learning how to use a map; using taxis to get to know the basic routes; establishing a definite landmark in each district and then linking these up; establishing 'use' areas very quickly and then spreading from these, and so on. These are all general habits of behaviour which can be applied deliberately. The operations include a mixture of approaches and there is quite a high risk of failure (like getting poor instructions when you ask the way), but the general operations provide a framework both for acquiring knowledge and for using a very little knowledge. In the other approaches, action can only follow after knowledge. In the general operations approach, action and knowledge go hand in hand. The general operations provide something definite to do instead of drifting round and hoping that eventually enough knowledge will accumulate.

Above all, once learned the general operations are applicable to new situations.

General operations and thinking

The knowledge approach to a subject is the content approach. Learn enough about the subject and the knowledge will do your thinking for you. The formulae approach may be compared to definite formulae situations where you learn to recognize the exact situation and then to plug in the appropriate formula. The method is effective, but it is restricted to those areas which can be dealt with in this way. The general operations approach is the one that is used in the CoRT Thinking programme, where an attempt is made to develop and practise some general operations that can be applied to different thinking situations.

Tools and abstraction

There are two ways of deriving general operations. The traditional way is to immerse pupils in 'thinking' situations and then to encourage them to abstract certain principles. These principles, abstracted under guidance, are then polished and put into a form general enough for use in other situations. This process is illustrated in diagram 21. In theory the system works well. In practice it does not. It is easy enough to provide interesting thinking situations. It is also easy enough to suppose that because a pupil is indeed *thinking* in such situations he must also be abstracting some general principles. What tends to happen is that the interest and the momentum of the content preclude any attention being paid to the thinking process itself. Moreover to make the required abstraction requires bright pupils and inspired teachers. Abstractions do not happen easily or naturally. Perhaps the greatest disadvantage of the method is that only a few limited principles can be abstracted in this way. They are abstracted over and over again, even though they may form only a small part of thinking. These tend to be concerned with the rules of evidence and the rules of logical inference. With hindsight it is quite easy to 'show' how any principle could be derived by abstraction from a situation, but showing something in this way is very different from actually doing it this way. You can show how a consideration of 'priorities' could have been abstracted from a certain thinking situation, but if no one ever does abstract this consideration the theoretical possibility is irrelevant.

Diagram 22 shows a different approach. Here the operations are created deliberately and independently as tools. There is no question of waiting for them to be abstracted. They are created artificially and offered in advance. A thinking situation is then provided for the use and practice of the tools so that the user may acquire some skill with them. In fact a variety of thinking

Diagram 21

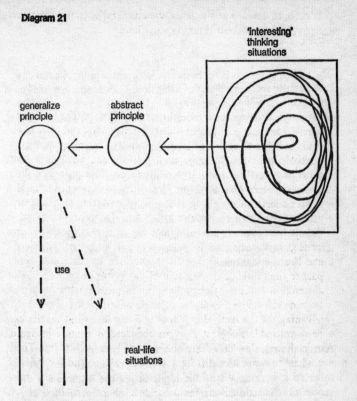

situations is provided so that attention may remain with the tool that is being used, rather than shifting to the subject matter of the thinking situation. The abstraction process is completely bypassed. The tools are created and applied. Practice in a variety of thinking situations builds up familiarity and skill in the use of the tool. This skill can now be applied when the tool is applied to real life. In this way the transfer problem can be solved. Skill is built into a transferable tool.

CoRT Tools

The CoRT approach is to crystallize different aspects of thinking into definite tools or objects of attention. Each lesson is based on one such tool. For example the general habit of trying to consider other people's viewpoint is crystallized into an 'OPV' lesson. It is often objected that such tools are artificial and even inappropriate. It is argued that there is a great deal of overlap and that the tools do not occupy areas that are psychologically or philosophically distinct. It is further argued that in many cases the so-called tools do no more than give a jargon name to a process that is well recognized anyway. Finally it is argued that the whole approach gives too tight a structure to thinking, which ought to flow freely.

All these arguments are valid, and indeed it is their very validity that makes the CoRT approach so necessary. We can take the main objections one by one.

Artificial

Artificial names or 'codes' are not used for every CoRT lesson, but where they are used it is for a definite purpose. You may have to make something unobvious for it to get the attention it deserves. Obvious things are far more difficult to teach than anything else. Everyone knows that it is a good thing to look at the advantages and disadvantages of an idea. But very few people actually do look at the advantages and disadvantages when it seems obvious at first glance that the idea is a good or bad one. Yet that is precisely the situation in which such an examination is most required. Borderline situations do often get a two-sided examination, but pre-judged situations do not. Since everyone knows about looking at the 'pros and cons', the best that the teacher can manage is exhortation or admonition – both of which are rather weak. But by creating the deliberate PMI tool (plus, minus and interesting points) the CoRT lesson creates a new area of atten-

Diagram 22

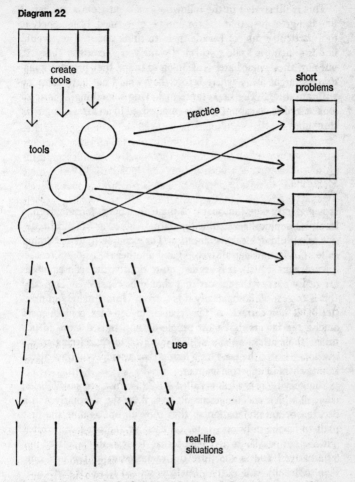

tion. Pupils can now look at the PMI in a definite manner and can use the process as a definite tool. The teacher now teaches the lesson about PMI. He can instruct the pupils to 'do a PMI' instead of just exhorting them not to be one-sided. There is something definite to look at and to do.

This is illustrated in the following comment from a teacher: 'I find it a great help that the thinking is objectified. I then apply it to a particular subject I want them to think about. They would find it difficult if I said to them: 'I want you to consider this . . .', but now they immediately cotton on to it and they produce something straight away where before they would not have come up with anything.' The importance of having something definite to look at and to do cannot be over-emphasized in an area as vague as thinking.

Overlap

It is perfectly true that many of the CoRT operations do overlap in a philosophical sense. But they are designed as practical tools, not as a philosophical classification. For example there is a lesson called CAF (consider all factors) and another called C&S (consequences and sequel). It is argued, quite rightly, that consequences are really part of the factors that should be considered. Logically this is correct. Philosophically it is correct. Unfortunately in practice it is not correct. A few people do consider consequences among the factors, but most people do not. Indeed most do not unless their *attention is specifically drawn* to considering consequences – hence the need for a lesson that attempts to draw attention to them in a specific manner.

Similarly there is a lesson called APC (alternatives, possibilities, choices) which encourages pupils to look at the alternatives in a decision or an explanation so that they do not assume the first path to be the only one. Later on there is another lesson called 'Find other ways'. It is claimed that this is also a search for 'alternatives' and is therefore the same lesson as the first one. Philosophically this is true, but this second lesson is concerned with the search for perceptual alternatives, for different ways of *looking* at something: is an industry a means of making profits, or a method of supplying goods, or a system for employing people and redistributing wealth? There is a practical distinction between the use of the word 'alternative' in: 'I am supposed to leave school next term, what alternatives do I have?' and in: 'I don't want you to look at this year in the factory as a training period but as a time in which you can think about what you really want – do you see this alternative way of looking at it?'

A problem does arise because our teaching habits are traditionally based on 'distinctions', on teaching from the boundary inwards, so that distinctions become crystallized into definitions of difference, whereas in CoRT the teaching moves from the centre outwards, with the result that a sharply established central point may have a region of overlap and uncertainty at its boundary. This point will be discussed in more detail later.

A certain amount of overlap is deliberate. Each lesson is short and some of the thinking processes are basic enough to enter into several lessons under different guises. The general policy is to produce a total picture by overlap rather than building up a hierarchy.

Structure

In the field of thinking there is an instinctive dislike of structure and jargon. It is felt that any structure confines or restricts thinking to tramlines. There is a mental image of a robot programmed to react to a series of jargon instructions. All this is contrasted with the free-flowing exploring mind in its untrammelled curiosity. This is somewhat idealistic. The free-flowing mind in practice is just as likely to indulge in wandering, waffle, drift and prejudice as in searching exploration. It is also likely to be confronted by a frightening void when asked to think about something: 'Where do I start? What do I do?'

The fear of structure arises from a failure to distinguish between restricting structures and liberating structures. Tracks, tramlines, rooms, cages, concepts can all be restricting structures. But a ladder, a hammer and a concept can all be liberating structures. A hammer enables you to hit nails in more easily. A cup enables you to drink a fluid. A ladder enables you to hang something high on the wall. All these structures are enabling rather than restricting. You do not have to use them, but if you want to they make it easier to do certain things. A key can be a restricting structure if it is used to lock someone in a room. It is also a liberating structure if he uses it to unlock the door of the room. A concept can be a restricting structure if it determines that we can look at something only in a fixed way. But it is a liberating structure in so far as it enables us to look at certain things at all, to use what we see or to communicate it.

Tools are liberating structures. They allow us to do things we could not otherwise have done – or at least they make them easier. In an absolute sense any opportunity is a restriction. If I give you a bicycle I am restricting your willingness to walk. If I give you an electric drill I am restricting your opportunity to use a hand drill. If I teach you to bypass prejudice I am restricting your ability to use prejudice. This is all philosophically true but not very practical – otherwise one would never do anything, because commitment to doing anything restricts one's freedom to do something else at that moment.

A comment from a headmistress illustrates the point: 'My teachers feared that it [CoRT] would teach children to think in tramlines. But it did not. On the contrary they surprised themselves with ideas they had not had before.'

The use and understanding of tools

There is an important distinction to be made between the use and understanding of tools. The distinction is important because most of education is geared to the principle that 'understanding' is all-important. We teach to the stage of 'understanding'. The emphasis is now on understanding mathematics rather than just being able to do it. The danger is that in teaching thinking tools (like the CoRT tools) the teacher may feel that it is enough if the pupils *understand* the tool and its purpose. This is far from enough. Practice in the use of the tool is far more important than understanding in this instance. Understanding is easy. Everyone understands about prejudice and about the need to consider other people's viewpoint. But such understanding does not help without the development of a skill and a habit. A carpenter can use a chisel without understanding too much about the type of steel involved or the importance of changes in the angle of the cutting edge. A metallurgist who understands all about the steel or a designer who understands, in theory, all about the angle of cutting edges may have less actual skill than the carpenter in the use of the chisel. Understanding is very helpful and we should aim towards it. But, where tools are concerned, it is no substitute for practice and use.

Attention-directors

The CoRT Thinking programme, which is used through the second part of this book as the practical basis for the discussion of teaching thinking as a skill, is mainly to do with perception. This is because most ordinary thinking takes place at the stage of perception rather than at that of processing – a matter that has been discussed at numerous points in this book.

When we are dealing with thinking we are dealing with perception.

When we are dealing with perception we are dealing with patterns.

When we are dealing with patterns we are dealing with attention.

When we are dealing with attention we have to use attention-directors.

That is why the CoRT Thinking tools end up as attention-directors. Attention flows along the patterns set up by our perception in order to handle our experience. In fact experience forms itself into patterns according to the immediate disposition and past experience of the mind that is perceiving it. We can passively allow attention to wander through experience as in the daydream type of thinking, or we can try to do something deliberate about attention. There are only two sorts of things we can do about attention. The first is to try to direct it by providing directions. The second is to try to direct it by providing destinations.

Directions and destinations

You can tell someone to go north or south. Or you can tell him to
stop at the first pub or petrol station or church. In the first case we
choose from our standard repertoire of directions. In the second
case we choose from our standard repertoire of destinations. In the
CoRT Thinking lessons, in order to allow attention thoroughly to
explore available experience, we create attention-directors that
may take the form either of directions or of destinations: 'I want
you to look in this direction,' or: 'I want you to look until you see
this'.

It is not easy to appreciate that destinations direct attention. A
young architecture student is asked to go and look at a terrace of
Georgian houses in Dublin. He comes back and says that they all
look 'very nice and very elegant'. He is unable to crystallize his
perception in any more definite way because he was unable to
direct his attention to the specific characteristics of Georgian architecture. With a lot of exposure and experience he might have
'noticed' these features for himself. But if they are 'noticed' for him
then he has something to direct his attention towards and he
comes to 'see' the features for himself. For instance he may have
his attention directed to the proportions, to the fanlights, to the
way the architraves are treated.

Many people have seen El Greco paintings in art galleries. They
can recognize the distinctive etiolated style. Yet not more than
one in a hundred will have noticed the very distinctive and
artificial manner in which the third and fourth fingers of the
hands of a holy person are usually widely separated. Once this
feature has been brought to someone's attention then, thereafter,
he cannot fail to notice it every time he sees an El Greco painting.

Attention-direction and patterns

Using the basic pattern notation that was developed earlier in the book, we can look at the twin processes of attention-directing.

In diagram 23 we see the standard track with the alternative track. Our attention would normally flow along the track from A to B, ignoring C. The material or pattern itself cannot provide us with a reason for directing attention along the track to C. We have to provide some *outside* reason for directing our attention along it. It is no use just making an effort of will to direct attention to C. We cannot make an effort to move towards C until we

Diagram 23

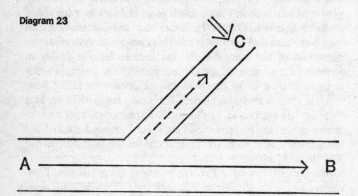

have noticed its existence. We have to set up an outside structure, an overriding pattern, an ego-pattern, which directs us to look in the C direction and see what we notice. In system terms this overriding pattern would be called a 'meta-system', since it is outside the first system. Similarly the attention-directors have to lie outside the ordinary information–experience patterns.

We can use the analogy of a child reaching the kerb. He wants to cross the road and so he crosses – without looking. It would not be much use instructing him: 'When you reach the kerb, if you see a car don't cross until the car has passed.' He would never see the car unless he looked for it. Instead we set up an elaborate 'Look left, look right, look left again' *drill* as a sort of overriding pattern. In other words we say: 'If you recognize this kerbside situation then, whatever other patterns of behaviour or attraction or action are in your mind, you must break off and go through this artificial performance to see if you generate anything you should react to.' Similarly a CoRT attention-directing tool would say 'Look in these directions to see what you can find – whether or not there is a natural reason or inclination to do so.'

In diagram 24 we see a different situation. Attention is gliding straight down the track from A to B. You want attention to pause at C in the same way that you might want a child to read a notice about swimming before plunging into the river. Only the notice does not actually exist. It is no use saying: 'Pause at C,' or 'Hold attention for a while at C,' because C does not exist. In order to get attention to pause at C we have to create C. In other words we have to create a destination or concept. In the Georgian example we introduced the concept of 'proportion', and in the El Greco

Diagram 24

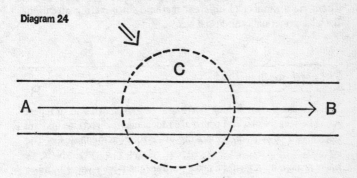

example we introduced the concept of 'finger separation' to hold up attention-flow. In the CoRT lessons we may create specific concepts, categories, boxes or labelled ways of looking at things.

The same effect could be reversed if we were to say (diagram 25) 'Do not stop at B but go on to C.' Again we would have to create the C concept.

The difference between these two basic processes is that the 'directions' belong to a super-pattern which is independent of the material itself. The 'destination' method of directing attention, is however, derived from the material.

Diagram 25

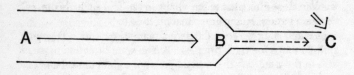

Types of CoRT tool

We can now look at the different ways in which the basic principles of attention-directing are applied in the CoRT lessons. There are a number of *different* methods for directing attention. Each basic method is discussed below.

The north-south method

You can ask a man to look north and to look south and to report what he sees. North and south are independent directions and are not related to what he is looking at or to what he may see. The compass points are an independent reference system which we have artificially set up in order to find out where we are and to provide a method for guiding our boats and our vision. We use the clock face in the same way. A biology teacher may ask his pupil, who is looking at a slide down a microscope, to 'look in the two o'clock position and tell me what you see.'

A thinker may not be in the habit of looking at the consequences of his decisions or suggestions. He is given explicit instructions to 'look in the direction of the consequences.' The instructions may be even more explicit: 'Look in the direction of the immediate consequences, then look in the direction of the medium-term consequences, finally look in the direction of the long-term consequences.' Instead of having to say all this the teacher just says: 'Do a C&S', which refers to the CoRT lesson in which these directions-for-looking are set out.

In another lesson the pupil is asked 'to look in the direction of the advantages or plus points; then in the direction of the dis-advantages or minus points; and finally in the direction of the interesting points.' As we have seen, more simply the operation is called a PMI.

Diagram 26 North-south method

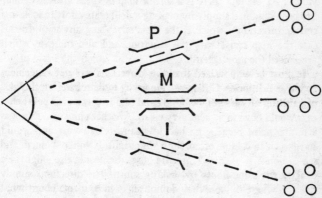

Diagram 26 illustrates how the definite directions are set up by the CoRT tool structure and the pupils are asked to look in these directions. What the pupil actually sees depends on his ability and experience. *But at least he has looked in that direction.* Often it is very easy to see something once you look in the right direction – but impossible to see it if you do not. In the experiment mentioned earlier, pupils were asked to say whether they thought it would be a good idea for all pupils to be given a wage for going to school. The idea seemed attractive and was judged to be so by one group.

But the other group, who did manage to look in the direction of the disadvantages, did not find it difficult to see them. In other experiments where a class has been asked to do a PMI on the suggestion, the disadvantages have become so obvious that the children have changed their minds.

Looking in a certain direction does not generate ideas, nor does it process information, nor is it difficult – it simply makes available to one's thinking a part of experience that might otherwise have been ignored.

In CoRT III there is an attention-director called ADI. This requires pupils in a conflict situation to 'look in the direction of the areas of Agreement, then in the direction of the areas of Disagreement, and finally in the direction of the areas of Irrelevance'. At the end there is a sort of map of these areas. The map has been obtained simply by making a deliberate effort to look in a certain direction – which is the basis of making any map. In this case the map can clarify the situation and also indicate which areas need the most attention.

It must be emphasized that the 'directions' are not judgement boxes or categories. Children were asked to do a PMI on the idea of painting all cars yellow. One child said it was a plus point that cars would have to be kept very clean. Another child said that was a minus point because he had to clean his dad's car and would have to clean it more often. Both were right. If you look north and see a house it is not a 'north-house'. Someone else might see exactly the same house by looking south. The directions simply tell you where to look: they do not make judgements about what is seen by looking in those directions. A child may offer as a minus point: 'Yellow cars would be harder to see and so there would be more crashes.' The teacher would correct this on a factual basis by saying that in fact yellow cars were easier to see, and the point might become a plus one. But the child was right to see that point by looking in the minus direction.

A series of such attention-directors (especially in CoRT I) encourages pupils to look in a wider sweep round a situation instead of rushing off after the obvious, short-term, egocentric, pre-judged line of thought.

The bird-watching method

During the war special plane-spotters were trained to recognize types of plane from their silhouettes even when they were a great distance off. Bird-watchers learn to recognize the characteristics of the different species so that they can spot them at once. This recognition process involves making a deliberate attempt to look for certain features. In learning to think we need to recognize

Diagram 27 Bird-watching method

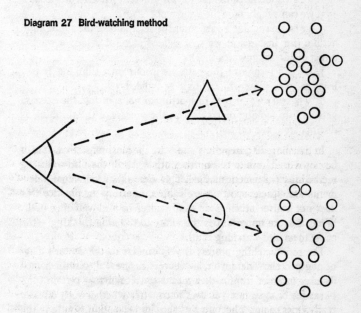

certain 'species' of thought: some of these species are well established but others have to be created deliberately. This is a use of attention-direction by creating destinations as is shown in diagram 27.

In the CoRT III lessons the pupils are given practice in spotting 'facts' and 'opinions'. They are also asked to pick out 'key' evidence. In other lessons they are asked to observe and recognize basic strategies for being wrong (unintentionally) such as 'exaggerate' or 'miss-out'. All these involve the bird-watching process.

This means having something to look for; making observations and judgements; getting better at the recognition process.

We can look at the purposes behind this bird-watching exercise as applied to thinking:

1. we can understand something about thinking from the patterns we are asked to pick out

2. we are motivated to look for the different patterns or species

3. we can simply note the occurrence

4. we can recognize a particular species and take the appropriate action: (for instance if we spot a 'key' piece of evidence we can direct our attack towards that)

5. we can recognize the patterns in our own thinking and so learn to avoid those which should be avoided

6. whatever we succeed in spotting or not spotting, the exercise gets us into looking objectively at the *process* of the thinking as distinct from the content

In the above list, items 4, 5 and 6 are the most important. It is to be noted that unlike the north-south method, the bird-watching method is a judgement method. This means that individual judgements and species-spotting are subject to errors. In practice this does not matter much more than it does in bird-watching itself. What is more important is the effort to examine thinking – the effort to go bird-watching at all.

The bird-watching process is very similar to the doctor's diagnosing process. The doctor, however, has 'created' certain named diseases in order to provide a means for recognizing certain combinations of symptoms. It does not matter whether such diseases really exist or not. They are packages for perception. Similarly the CoRT 'species' are not meant to be philosophical definitions of aspects of thinking, but convenient perception packages.

The apple-boxing method

This could be called the 'oblique attention method'. It has certain similarities to the bird-watching method but enough distinction for it to be kept separate. In the bird-watching method we saw that a doctor wanted to identify the 'species' of disease so that he could start the right treatment. Similarly the pupil would want to recognize certain patterns or 'species' of thinking so that he could take appropriate action. This element of recognition-for-appropriate-action is entirely missing from the apple-boxing method.

The other element of the bird-watching method that it encouraged the pupil to examine the thinking in a detached and observant manner. This element is present in the apple-boxing method. Indeed it is the very basis of the method.

A farmer asks his somewhat lazy son to separate a pile of apples into two boxes. One box is for the bigger apples and the other box is for the smaller apples. At the end of the day the farmer returns and finds that the apples have been sorted into the two boxes. Apples that were badly bruised or damaged by birds or insects have been put aside in a separate pile. The farmer thanks his son for the excellent work and then proceeds to fill sacks indiscriminately from both boxes, so that in the end each sack contains both large and small apples in random proportions. The boy is furious and believes it to have been some trick to test his willingness to work. What was the use of sorting out the apples into large and small if they are then going to be mixed together again?

The farmer explains that it was no trick. He wanted each individual apple to be examined carefully so that the bad ones could be thrown out. The large and small boxes were only an *oblique device* to get the apples examined *properly*. Had he asked the boy directly to throw out the bad apples then each apple would not have been examined. The boy would have looked through them quickly – looking only for the obviously bad apples and never examining those which seemed sound. So the two boxes were an oblique way of getting attention paid to the apples. The final categories were totally unimportant, as is shown in diagram 28.

In the CoRT V lessons the same oblique method is used. The value of the final categories is not totally absent but varies from lesson to lesson. For instance the distinction between 'shooting questions' and 'fishing questions' is a useful one. On the other hand the distinction between a 'small guess' and a 'big guess' is very difficult to make in a definite and useful manner. Similarly the distinction between a 'high value' and a 'low value' is also

Diagram 28   Apple-boxing method

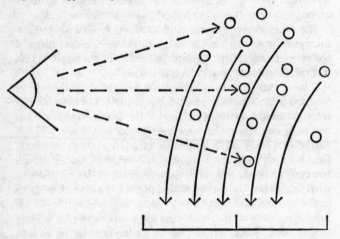

difficult to make, even though it is important. What is really important is that guesses should be recognized and examined directly to see how well founded they are, and that values should also be examined carefully in order to set up some order of priorities.

It is unfortunate that our minds prefer category boxes to 'flagpoles' that mark the end of a spectrum. It is easier to ask pupils to judge a value and to put it into a 'high value' box or a 'low value' box than to say where the value fits on a spectrum running from very high value to very low value. So for convenience the oblique boxing method is used – but on the understanding that what is really intended is a close examination of the values involved.

The isolation method

This method is very ordinary and obvious and part of everyday teaching. It is a matter of 'isolating' an attention area which is normally part of such a swift flow of attention that it gets too little attention. For example when we start to think about something it is obvious that we have started to think about something and so we pay little attention to where we start. By deliberately isolating the process of 'starting' we hold attention in that area, so that we can consider how to start rather than what follows next. Similarly when we are looking at something it is obvious that we are looking at something. But if we draw back and isolate the process of 'focus' (as in CoRT II), then we can examine what it is that we are really looking at. When we come to the end of our thinking there may be a definite conclusion, or it may tail off. If, however, we isolate this area of 'conclusion' we can then examine what it is we have arrived at, even if it is not a definite judgement. In the 'conclusion' lesson a whole range of possible conclusions is listed. It is not so important that the pupil should use or remember these as that he should realize that there are different sorts of conclusion and that if he pays direct attention to this area he may see that there really is a conclusion to his thinking, even if at first sight there did not appear to be one.

Diagram 29 illustrates how the isolation method of attention-direction attempts to hold attention in an area that is usually passed through almost automatically. If you pick up a cup it is natural that you should grasp the handle. But that does not mean that you pay much attention to the handle. It is necessary for someone to say: 'Pause and look at the handle' or: 'Pause and look at the way you are lifting the cup' for any attention to paid to this area.

Diagram 29   Isolation method

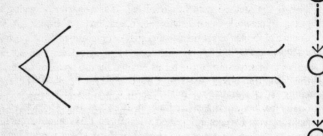

There are similarities between the isolation method and the bird-watching method in so far as the pupil is being asked to look at something definite. In the bird-watching method, however, a phenomenon is deliberately created in order to be the subject of attention. In the isolation method it is more a matter of isolating something which happens naturally and holding attention there in an unnatural manner.

As we have seen in previous sections, the two main problems with attention are that it does not always go in the direction we should like and that it does not pause where we should like it to pause. The natural flow and timing of attention are controlled by experience, not by the purpose of the thinking. In order to increase skill in thinking we have to achieve some sort of control over attention-flow. The isolation method is an attention-director because it directs attention back to an area that has been skimmed through too rapidly.

It is quite easy to understand the isolation method but rather difficult to teach it, since pupils become impatient with having to pay attention to something they consider to be automatic.

The framework method

This is the method used in CoRT VI. It is a matter of trying to put a framework to the deliberate operation of thinking. A sequence of 'boxes' is set up as suggested in diagram 30a. Each box is an attention area. Each box has to be filled by thinking about the problem or situation in the terms defined by the box. For example the 'attention-boxes' used in CoRT VI are: Purpose (the endpoint, what you want to end up with, aim, objective); Input (the scene, the setting, the ingredients, the factors to be considered, the information available); Solutions (alternative solutions or suggestions for solving the problem); Choice (the choice of decision stage in which one of the alternative suggestions is chosen); Operations (the action steps by means of which the solution is put into effect). Each box holds attention on a specific thinking task. Instead of trying to cover all areas thinking is directed towards just one area at a time. The boxes are of course artificial and any other type of box would do as well. These basic boxes provide deliberate 'stages' in thinking about something.

Diagram 30   Framework method

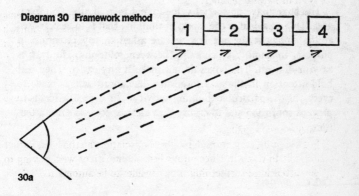

30a

Each of the basic stages can be elaborated and this elaboration is suggested by further boxes as shown in diagram 30b. These further boxes do not have to be filled because they are in the nature of elaborating tools which are used only if 'further thinking' is required at that point. For example one tool is 'Target' and this is concerned with focusing precisely on some point. The next tool is 'Expand' and this means elaborating in breadth, depth and alternatives on that point. The 'Contract' tool invites a conclusion or summary.

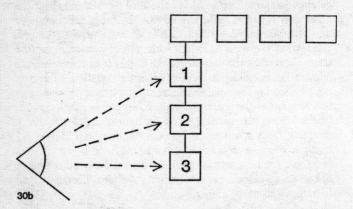

30b

The boxes have no special value-except to hold attention in an area. This area defines the aspect of thinking that is to be practised at that moment. In one box we are asked to pay attention to purpose, in another to choosing between solutions. The task is easy or difficult. The boxes do not make it any easier. They just hold attention in the area to ensure that an attempt is made to carry out the particular thinking activity. The over-all effect is to prevent confusion and to ensure that each aspect gets some attention.

Process models

Most of the attention-directors serve to direct attention to areas. It is just as easy to direct attention to processes such as 'analyse' or 'compare' (both from CoRT II). In fact attention is being directed to a model of the process: 'This is how analysis works, let's see if we can use that process on this situation.' In effect, many of the processes are themselves attention-directors. The 'compare' process

Diagram 31 Process model method

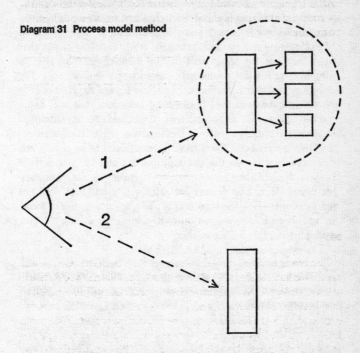

directs attention to those features which two situations have in common and also to the features which differ. The 'analyse' process serves to direct attention away from the total situation and towards the component features.

This particular attention-directing method is illustrated in diagram 31.

Summary

All teaching may be said to be a matter of attention-directing. The teaching of thinking is almost entirely a matter of attention-directing, since there is no new knowledge-content. In the exploration of experience for a purpose, attention tends to follow tracks that have been set up by experience, by emotion and by narrow interests (egotistical, immediate consequences and so on). The only way to direct attention over a wider field of experience is to set up an outside method of directing attention: that is to say a method which can be applied from the outside to any situation instead of arising from within the situation itself. The attention-directors are artificial. They have to be artificial to be of any use. They are imposed on the thinking process and are not derived from analysis of the process: they are operating devices, not passive descriptions. The devices are often crude but that does not matter. Quite often the intention is oblique – that is to say something is done in one way in order to achieve something else (for example the apple-boxing method).

The various methods used are listed here:

The north-south method: setting up an external reference system to direct attention towards certain things such as other people, consequences and so on

The bird-watching method: the spotting of certain phenomena or patterns used in thinking, for example the different ways of being right or wrong

The apple-boxing method: the sorting of things into categories with the oblique intention that this sorting will lead to close examination of the things themselves, as in the examination of values and guesses

The isolation method: isolating certain obvious and automatic areas so that they will get more direct attention, as at the 'start' of thinking

The framework method: setting up and using a checklist of attention-areas which are set up ahead of the situation; each attention-area or box is then filled in turn from the situation

The process model method: directing attention to some basic processes as distinct from areas: setting up models of the processes and then trying to apply them, as in 'analyse' and 'compare'.

It must of course be said that setting up an outside system for directing attention does not mean that it will automatically be used. A thinker may still prefer to follow the attention-flow set up by ideas, experience and emotion and may ignore the external system. Alternatively a thinker may use some of the external devices but by no means all. Fortunately there is considerable benefit to be obtained even by the use of only some of the attention-directing methods. For example the use of the PMI alone can improve thinking by avoiding instant judgement.

It must also be said that simply understanding the attention-directing devices is not enough. They are very easy to understand. Understanding alone will never lead to use. Use can come only from habit and habit can come only from practice.

Preliminary discussion

The preliminary discussion arises when it is first suggested, in general or in a staff common room, that thinking might be taught directly as a skill. When I first made a suggestion of this sort in the columns of *The Times Educational Supplement* there was a good deal of correspondence about the philosophical and moral aspects of the idea. Thinking is so very wide a subject that it is possible to have unlimited discussions of this sort without ever arriving at any conclusion, since everyone is talking about a different thing and virtually no one is talking about the *particular* approach to thinking that is intended. To mention the word 'thinking' is to unleash philosophical speculation and moral hesitancy. (Any attempt to do anything to or for the mind is always suspect.) On the whole these discussions are interesting and even fascinating but have nothing to do with the teaching of thinking as a skill.

The more focused reactions to the suggested teaching of thinking usually take one or other of the following practical forms.

A priori rejection of the idea

'Thinking is a process we seem to have managed quite capably so far without it being labelled.'

'You can't teach people to think – only things about which to think.'

'I happen to like the old curriculum because we are used to it – let other schools experiment.'

'Most of the other staff haven't heard of it and if they have it's one of those funny things and they don't want it here thank you very much.'

'It is not a good idea for everyone to think. In a diversified society someone will inevitably turn up ideas and argue them – rather than everyone thinking for himself.'

It must be said at once that the value of thinking itself, or the value of everyone thinking for himself, or the usefulness of improving thinking, are more matters of general belief than of rational argument.

Why is thinking a good thing?

Why is it good for everyone to think?

Why is learning to think more broadly a good thing?

These questions can be answered and argued and I enjoy doing so in the terms outlined at the beginning of the book. But you cannot convince anyone by argument because the issue is moral, not rational. If you really believe it is better for an élite to do the thinking and everyone else to do what he or she is told you have an argument. If you really believe that thinking only confuses and that prejudice is a direct and useful response then you also have an argument.

On the other hand the generally accepted belief that thinking, being the exploration of experience for a purpose, is a biologically useful function is self-evident to those who find it so.

Request for proof and evaluation

The type of person who makes this request is basically doubtful or suspicious of the idea of teaching thinking as a skill. The request for proof and evaluation would seem to be a very normal one, except that any proof that is offered is always deemed to be insufficient.

'What is the evaluation which shows that children can be taught to think more than they are at the moment?'

'We would like to think that we are teaching them to think, but instead of doing this we may be handing them a pre-package.'

Hard data are judged to be irrelevant or the result of teaching the test. Soft data in the form of teachers' comments are judged to be biased or subjective. These objections are valid. But a request to show that teaching thinking has changed the life of a pupil over the succeeding twenty years is a form of evaluation that could not be applied to subjects such as literature, languages, geography, science or history. Certainly learning to read and write matters very much. But virtually all else is taught in the belief that greater knowledge about the world is a good thing – though we have no direct proof for saying so. In a very few cases learning a foreign language may lead to a job in that country, but this would not justify teaching the language to thousands of other children.

There is often a feeling that teaching thinking ought to improve performance in other subjects rather than in real life. There is evidence that it improves performance in other thinking areas (such as English essays), but in knowledge-bound subjects it is more difficult to show an effect.

General interest

'It has always surprised me how easy it is to convince teachers that there is value in doing this work.'

This comment from a research worker does reflect the true state of interest in teaching thinking as a skill. Many teachers have always wanted to do so. They have felt that underlying the different subjects there must be a basic thinking skill that might be transferable to life outside school. So the idea is not new to them. They may disagree with the particular approach suggested, in fact they might disagree with any approach suggested, but nevertheless they accept the basic concept. Many of them are eager to explore what purports to be a practical and definite framework for teaching thinking directly.

'This course slightly modifies both the processes and the terminology but proves a useful aid in achieving what we were trying to achieve anyway. I don't think it greatly modifies, it clarifies, provides useful examples and interesting terminology.'

'What I like is the definite framework. Instead of just muddling along one can set out to do a C A F or P M I or whatever.'

'We do it all the time'

This is undoubtedly true in some cases, and partly true in others. All teachers teach some thinking. It would be absurd to expect a teacher to deny that he taught thinking. But teaching thinking directly as a transferable skill is a different matter from asking children to 'think' about the content of their lesson. As in the first case there is no room for argument here. If a teacher feels that he, personally, teaches his subject in such a way as to create a transferable thinking skill applicable to very different matters, then there is no way of convincing him otherwise.

Special reasons

'The way it was proposed it was not just thinking as such. It was also linked with a certain amount of guidance for some of the less able, careers discussion and so on.'

'It is perhaps an ignoble motive but it is very useful for the head to have to hand material which no one else has, because that means that he can go into a class and sparkle without having someone come just after and say: "You have just done the seventeenth century, which I was going to do next week".'

'I felt that the CoRT work could help us to combine the traditional and the progressive.'

'In these open-ended discussion subjects we have always felt a certain amount of drift – following on where interest takes us. We were looking for some sort of structure, a cognitive structure if you like, to hold things together.'

'The point about discussion skills caused me to look at CoRT in the first place, in the sense that in a fully operational open-plan lower school you deal with individuals on a one-to-one basis. And then suddenly in the third year you say: 'Now you are a class, work together, speak together, stand up and express an opinion.' It seemed that CoRT was a good way of getting a class together to talk about specific things, and of giving us some material around which we could work – and each of us in the teaching team would be doing the same thing.'

Many of these special-case reasons can be quite different from the basic intention of teaching thinking as a skill. As we shall see later, the programme is often used to teach English as a foreign language. In an oblique way, however, those who put them forward do realize that thinking is a basic skill.

Practical points

The preliminary discussion then moves on to such practical points as the following:

most appropriate age or ability level
subject area or timetable slot
amount of time required per week, number of weeks
teacher training required
effect on other subject areas
general effect, testing and evaluation procedures

'What's the time investment before we can see definite results?'

'Could we spare Joan to do the whole of the first year so that it is gradually being fed upwards through the whole school?'

'What aim would the pupils see in it? How do we sell it to them?'

'Where do we bring it in? If it is that valuable ought we to leave it until year four?'

These practical aspects will be covered in subsequent sections.

Expectations

As we shall see later the expectations of teachers and staff at this stage can determine the success or failure of the project. If expectations are set too high then disappointment is inevitable. The initial rush of enthusiasm on the part of teachers and pupils will be impossible to maintain. If there are very precise expectations as to what the course will achieve these may also be disappointed, unless they are connected to previous experience of the programme. On the other hand a tentative, hesitant approach will be unable to overcome awkwardness and obstacles.

As might be expected, a number of *a priori* judgements are made at this stage.

'The handbook says that the programme covers a wide age-range. I don't see how any material can cover that wide a range.'

'Isn't it a framework which by encouraging detachment can remove the emotional element which is also important in thinking?'

'This is I think CoRT's great attraction. Its applicability to a thousand and one problems.'

Age, ability and background

The most basic practical questions concern the age, ability and background of the pupils who might be expected to benefit from the thinking lessons. In many subject areas it would be easy to answer this question, since the material has been designed specifically for a particular age and ability bracket. This is not the case with the CoRT Thinking lessons for three reasons:

The peculiar nature of thinking as a subject.

The way the material is produced and the deliberate development strategy of allowing interested teachers at all levels of age and ability to use the material.

Because it is easy for teachers to adapt the basic framework to suit their own classrooms.

Thinking is not a knowledge subject. Therefore there is no hierarchy of knowledge which requires that a pupil should know the basic material before he is able to understand the more complicated material. Each of the processes crystallized in the CoRT lessons stands parallel to the others. It is possible to pick out different processes and teach them separately. It is possible to change the order and to teach later processes even if the earlier ones have not been learned.

The basic processes of thinking are the same at any age. The older and more able child may be able to use the processes more skilfully and to weave more knowledge and more subtlety into the use of the processes, but the basic process is the same. It is true that younger children do have difficulty with some of the processes. For example young children (up to eleven years old) find it very difficult to think in the future. As a result the lesson which is concerned specifically with looking at the future consequences of an action becomes difficult to teach:

'They are just not able to think in the future.'

'It was quite beyond them to think of the future consequences of the robot example.'

'They have conceptual problems with the future.'

As a result the teacher would simplify this lesson so that it dealt first with the 'immediate consequences' of an action and then with all the 'later consequences', instead of trying to consider immediate, short term, medium term and long term consequences.

Teachers claim that younger children have problems with the more abstract concepts. As a result in the PMI lesson the teacher would deal only with the plus (good) and minus (bad) points. This is probably justified, but there is a danger that a teacher *presupposes* that a child will not be able to deal with a particular concept or situation on the grounds that he himself has some slight difficulty and hence the child must have more difficulty. In some cases, however, the child may have less difficulty than the adult, because he is less confused by other concepts. As we shall see later, it is a bad mistake to suppose that children's interests or abilities are limited to what seems 'childlike'.

Trigger-material

Just as the basic thinking processes are the same at any age, so it is possible to choose practice items which can also be used at any age. This is because the items serve as 'trigger-material'; that is to say the item serves to set off the knowledge or experience which the pupil has stored in his mind. The thinking then deals with this knowledge. Just as the pressure on the trigger is independent of the charge in the gun, so the triggering problem may be the same and yet the sophistication of the thinking that is set off will vary with the age or ability of the thinker.

For example the suggestion that people should wear badges indicating their mood can be tackled at different levels of sophistication:

You might have to keep changing the badge all the time.
You could know who to avoid.
Would people be honest about their moods or just cheat?
Suppose you forget to change it round?

No one would talk to a person in a bad mood but that may be what she needs most.
Would the badges show just good, bad or what other moods?
A person might not think he was in a bad mood but others might – who decides what badge he should wear?

Is it important to know another person's mood?
It may be useful or good training to force yourself to disguise your mood.
Wouldn't it be very self-indulgent?
How much information do we get anyway about moods from tone of voice, facial expression, reaction and so on.

From the fun level to the involved psychological level the item can work as an opportunity to practise thinking. The ideas that turn up are not important. What is important is the thinking process that is practised in turning up the ideas. It is this peculiarity of thinking as a subject which makes it possible to produce material which can be used across a wide level of ages and abilities.

Adaptation

The youngest age group being taught the CoRT lessons are five-year-olds at Sunday schools run by the Unitarian Church in Britain. The oldest group are probably the IBM executives in France, who are using thinking lessons as a method for learning English and learning to think in English. These are extremes. In general the lessons have been used with primary-school children from the age of eight (more usually nine) up to sixth form and further-education students aged seventeen.

On the ability scale the lessons have been used with remedial groups and with groups with IQs as low as 80. At the other end of the scale the lessons have been used with very high-ability groups (IQs of 140) and even with gifted children. Some of these uses have been experimental and have arisen from the interest of a particular teacher who has wanted to explore the situation.

'This has given remedial children new confidence. They find that though they may not produce all the factors produced by the others they can still come up with new factors [in the CAF lesson] that no one else has thought of. You can see them grow in confidence.'

The background variety has been as great. The CoRT Thinking programme has been used in élite, highly selective public schools (in Britain) and in schools in areas considered so deprived that they are classified as 'educational priority areas'. In one school in the second group 80 per cent of the pupils came from coloured immigrant families. The socio-economic backgrounds of the pupils has varied as much as the character of the school (secondary modern, grammar school, comprehensive, college of further education). Within the school itself there has been a range of attitudes from authoritarian to exploratory, from traditional to progressive. What has been especially interesting is that the idea of teaching thinking directly as a skill has been taken up as much by the traditional schools as by the progressive ones. It has not been regarded as something 'new and liberating' but as something matter-of-fact and practical.

Although the basic processes and material are applicable across this wide range of ages, abilities and backgrounds, it must be obvious that in some cases individual teachers have to do their own adaptation. For example, with younger pupils the teacher may have to simplify the processes and omit some of them. He may also have to select the practice items and adapt them to the interest level of his pupils. He may have to provide some of his own practice items so that they can be of topical interest to the pupils: 'They prefer practical items like what to do if you want to cross the road . . .')

It should be mentioned here that many teachers presuppose that certain items must be too complicated or remote for younger children. Yet our experience is that children in the nine-to-twelve age group are ready to tackle just about any problem. I have had groups of ten-year-olds discussing for three-quarters of an hour, without supervision, the ultimate political question of whether people should be paid according to their needs or according to how hard they work. I have had other groups discussing week-end prisons for minor offenders. Most teachers would consider such problems far too 'adult' for such an age group. As a general principle the interest or thinking ability of children is almost always underestimated, because we equate thinking with knowledge. One teacher doubted whether the practice item on lending money would be of interest to his class of eight-year-olds, so he asked how many of them had lent money in the last month. About three-quarters of the hands went up.

Many primary-school teachers have commented that the material is not designed for younger children: that the printing ought to be larger and that there ought to be more pictures. Some of these comments are justified. But there is a major dilemma here. It is customary to make material for younger children so colourful that they get involved in it. This creates a problem in two ways. Firstly, if the children get too involved in the material then their attention remains focused on the material alone and it is difficult to focus it on the actual thinking process that is the subject of the lesson. It is *not enough* that children should be thinking of something and generally having an interesting time – there is a specific thinking process to be practised. This battle between content interest and process practice constitutes the basic dilemma that will be discussed in more detail later in connection with the problems that arise in teaching thinking as a subject. The second problem is that if the material is too well produced and too appropriate, the teacher will make no effort to run the lesson in her own way or to produce topical practice items. With younger children this personal adaptation by the teacher is much more important than pre-adapted material.

With older and more able children the adaptation often has to go in the opposite direction. The pupils will tend to be superficial and to assume that if they produce any answer it will do, since there are no finite answers. The teacher has to demand a much greater degree of sophistication and has to insist that the pupils go beyond the superficial. The teacher may also want to bring in practice items and topics from other subject areas. The teacher demands speed, briskness and competence. He has to emphasize that understanding the lesson is only a tiny part of it (understanding the lesson is easy) and that the main part is practising the ability to use the thinking process fluently and precisely – and knowing when to use it. With the older groups and the more able groups, superficiality and conceit are the major problems. Pupils who have always prided themselves on being clever throughout their school careers are apt to believe they are excellent at thinking, because in the narrow confines of knowledge subjects they function well. More important is the effect of many years' exposure to knowledge subjects in which there is something to learn (and there are right answers). The change to a process subject in which there is something to *do* can be awkward. What is even more awkward is that the pupils are used to 'difficult' things and feel that easy things can be answered adequately in a superficial way. It is quite difficult to get them to use an 'easy' process powerfully and in depth. The content/process dilemma is also a problem with older age groups who enjoy gossip-type discussion sessions.

Motivation

The motivation level of the pupils is set almost entirely by the teacher. The teacher has to give status to the subject. The teacher has to adapt the material. The teacher has to create a sense of achievement in the lessons. The teacher has to introduce variety and topicality. It must be remembered that only 'content' can be interesting in itself. 'Process' is made interesting by the way it is handled by the teacher. The teaching problems that arise are discussed in detail in a later section.

Pupils in the nine-to-twelve age group are usually well motivated. They enjoy thinking. They enjoy playing with ideas. They enjoy thinking about almost anything. Older children are more inhibited. Their thinking is more bound up with their ego and classroom status. They want to be right. They want to show how bright they are. They want to know if the subject matter is relevant or if there is going to be an exam.

Summary

Because of the nature of thinking as a subject, and because of the CoRT approach, it is possible to produce a programme that is usable – with considerable teacher adaptation – over a wide range of ages and abilities. It is too early to say at which age the material will have the most benefit or be easiest to use. Too much depends on the interest and ability of the teacher. The preferred age range would, however, be ten, eleven, twelve and thirteen. Thinking would be taught as a foundation subject in this age bracket. It could be used as a bridge subject between primary and secondary schools. That is to say some work would be done in the primary school and this would be repeated in greater depth and extended in the secondary school.

Intention

The idea of teaching thinking as a skill seems sensible enough. This can be a danger because it can mean that the subject is tried in an off-hand way. The success of the subject in any particular school depends first on the 'intention' with which it is used and then on the teacher who is teaching it.

In one school the headmaster was very interested in developing the subject in his school. The teacher to whom the task was delegated was somewhat less interested and in one lesson he simply scattered the first half-dozen CoRT lesson pamphlets on a table and asked the pupils to work through them before they could get on with their model aircraft building. In another school the thinking period was taken from the art period, which had always been the most popular lesson – with disastrous results. Sometimes the thinking lessons are used to plug a spare three-quarters of an hour for which no one else has found a use. With exceptional teachers even these off-hand uses can work, but on the whole the subject never gets a chance to be taken seriously by the pupils if treated in this manner.

It is difficult for a head to delegate a teacher to take the subject if the teacher is not really interested in doing so. On the other hand there are no subject boundaries. If a teacher is interested it does not matter whether the teacher comes from geography, physics, history, English or any other subject.

The token approach also tends to be ineffectual. The token approach is when a school feels that it ought to do something about this 'new' subject but rather wishes it would go away and not complicate timetabling. As a result a token effort is made to try the subject – in the hope that it will soon prove unsuitable and so can be dropped.

The 'with-it' approach seems very different but is not. Some heads or teachers rush to try anything new because it seems to offer excitement and they like to feel in the vanguard of educational matters. The lessons are tried, with enthusiasm, but if the subject fails to catch fire it is soon dropped. There is little determination to explore the best way of teaching the subject and of overcoming the obstacles. Instead of adaptation the teacher often takes over the subject and teaches it as a 'discussion' subject, which pays little heed to the processes that are supposed to be practised.

The special-interest approach has been mentioned in a previous section. This is where a head or teacher has a special reason for using the CoRT programme. This reason may or may not be aligned with the purpose behind the programme. Nevertheless this approach can be very successful.

Some people do not enjoy thinking at all. Others enjoy thinking about things but do not enjoy thinking about thinking. There is no natural reason why anyone should enjoy the CoRT Thinking lessons – except as an opportunity to think and to have your thinking listened to. Most people, teachers and pupils, acknowledge the purpose and usefulness of the lessons, but wild enthusiasm is the exception. And so it should be. The lessons should be tackled in a sober, matter-of-fact manner. An understanding of them and an enjoyment of them develop gradually. Pupils gradually acquire skill and enjoy using it. It does not happen in a flash. Indeed, the teacher is usually uncertain of himself until he has gone through the programme with one class. The second time round he knows better how to tackle the subject.

For all these reasons it is not much use trying the subject in an off-hand way and hoping that it will catch fire and so establish itself. There has to be a serious intention which will carry the teacher over the initial awkwardness. It is the serious intention that will enable the teacher to develop his own style of teaching the material.

It must also be mentioned that a hesitant or tentative approach on the part of the teacher: 'Let's see how this goes' communicates itself to the pupils. This approach may be all right in a content subject where the content itself provides a sufficient momentum. But in a 'process' subject like thinking the teacher has to maintain the pace himself. He must lead from in front – not from behind.

It is because teacher motivation is so very important to the success of the programme that a serious intention to teach thinking as a skill is so necessary. Attempts to 'dabble' in the subject are unlikely to be successful.

There is a difference between a 'trial' run and a 'development' run. In the trial run the attitude is: 'Let's try this and see if it works'. In the development run the attitude is: 'Let's see how we can *make* this work.' It is the second attitude that is most appropriate to the teaching of thinking as a subject. This is because the material only provides a framework and it is the teacher who has to make it work. To sit back and expect the framework to teach the subject is useless. Conversely the framework provides the teacher with a practical opportunity to teach thinking as a skill and to exercise his teaching skills in a way that is not possible in most other subject areas.

Timetable

No matter how worthwhile a subject is or how valuable it is perceived to be, there is a practical point which ultimately determines its fate: the timetable. By definition the timetable is full. It is crowded. Anything new has to displace something else. Where there are exams to be studied for and syllabuses to be completed the pressure is even greater. In view of this difficult timetable problem it is perhaps surprising how many schools have been able to try out the CoRT programme. The response is no indication of the value of that programme, but it is an indication of the willingness of schools to treat seriously the idea of teaching thinking directly as a skill. The various methods of timetabling the subject are indicated below. These methods indicate not the ingenuity of the school timetablers but the perceived placing of the subject.

Foundation subject

Several new schools have timetabled CoRT thinking as a foundation subject across all classes for the first and second year of secondary education. This sort of timetabling is of course easier with a new school, which starts with a blank sheet. Other schools are attempting to do the same. Junior or primary schools often find it possible to use CoRT lessons with all their older pupils.

Special subject

Where a particular teacher is interested in the programme, the subject is taught as a special subject in its own right to one or two classes. This is also the case when a school is experimenting with the subject before deciding on a fuller use.

Option subject

Some schools have an option system – especially at sixth-form level. CoRT Thinking can conveniently be used as one of the options. It might seem that an unknown subject would be unlikely to attract many choices. This does not seem to be the case, and many pupils choose 'thinking' because it seems an interesting subject. Some find that it does not match up to their expectations.

Examination subject

This is not yet a definite use. Many schools have suggested that the subject ought to give rise to a school-leaving exam because then it would be much easier to provide a timetable slot for it. This creates something of a dilemma. If the subject was turned into just another examination subject it would be taken by a few pupils but would lose its foundation position with all pupils at a lower age – and indeed its various uses elsewhere in the school. The matter is under consideration. Some schools are pushing ahead with plans to make it an examinable subject. A new exam called General Thinking Skills (GTS) may be set up.

Special-group subject

The raising of the school-leaving age in England created a group of pupils without an already established curriculum. Some schools have been trying the CoRT material as a subject in this area. Other schools are using the programme with special non-academic pupils who are not part of the examination streams on the grounds that an improved skill in thinking should be of use to them.

In the English department

This is by far the most common use. The English department has no formalized content and so it is easy to introduce new material. The emphasis in the English department is on process not on content, so the teaching style is well suited to the subject. There is clearly a very close connection between communication and thinking. Thinking itself provides an interesting subject area for practising language skills. If pupils are going to talk or write about something they might as well be thinking at the same time. In terms of teacher interest, teacher style, pupil expectations and process orientation this seems an excellent placement for the CoRT lessons.

'I started using CoRT quietly as a means of teaching conversation – then I noticed that the children were enjoying thinking and certain children were benefiting greatly. The ideas they produced were entertaining, interesting and useful.'

It has often been noted by teachers that the effect of doing the CoRT lessons usually turns up first in the English essays. This is not surprising, because this is one of the very few areas in the whole school curriculum in which free (not content-based) thinking is allowed. This close relationship between essays and thinking has been another reason for putting CoRT into the English department.

The pupils immediately said, 'What a good idea the PMI is for getting essay plans out.' I had been doing this in English and of course all the lessons in CoRT I can be applied in this way to the English lessons. There is a further advantage in that quite a considerable part of the curriculum is given over to English lessons – so there is more room within which to introduce the new subject. Naturally the thinking lessons can also be used for practising reading and writing as well as for speaking. In fact some teachers feel they even have a place in literature.

I know this teacher who takes the CoRT pack into her literature course about once a month – as a basis for getting her pupils to look at things and think about them.

Of course there are dangers involved in placing the CoRT lessons in the English department: 'I taught the CoRT lessons as part of the English lessons because I had to. It was the only time I had. I would not envisage doing it like this if I did not have to, because it tends to disappear without trace into the English department as yet another bit of spoken English.'

As part of religious instruction and moral education

This seems another natural timetable placement. Many of the lessons are seen to have a direct relevance to this area: looking at consequences, assessing priorities, considering other people's views, decisions, planning and so on. In general the relationship between thinking and behaviour is not difficult to perceive. Where this subject area is no longer based on formal content-teaching there is a growing need for discussion and thinking formats. The CoRT programme can fit in here. The programme has also been used in association with other, more specific, moral-education programmes. In one school the teacher was planning to use the CoRT lessons as a foundation for moral discussion sessions, but was forbidden to do so by the school inspector on the grounds that thinking had nothing to do with moral education. But that would seem to be a minority view.

As a core subject in integrated studies or interdisciplinary inquiry

With these teaching methods the pupils range across subject boundaries to consider topics or themes from a wide angle. The learning process consists of collecting and integrating material from a variety of sources (the resource centre). In some cases pupils have tended to collect the information and to present it without doing too much thinking about it. The CoRT lessons are seen as providing a cognitive structure which might serve as a 'core' for information-collecting. For instance a boy had done a project on buses and presented his material to the teacher. The teacher, who had done some of the CoRT lessons with the boy, asked him to go away and do a PMI on what would happen if all seats were removed from buses. This he did. The teacher comments that without some cognitive structure such as this she would simply have given the pupil another 'information' subject to seek out.

'We've made interdisciplinary inquiry into integrated humanities now and you can see it's entirely sociological, history and geography. It's very much more structured and the value of CoRT will be far more apparent because of the structure.'

It should be noted that certain information skills required in these subject areas (extracting information from figures, precise writing and so on) are distinct from the 'thinking' skills developed in the CoRT material.

As a core in social studies

Social studies tend to be something of a discussion area. The intention is often to make the pupils more aware of the world around them. Teachers in this area have observed that a pupil may demonstrate some thinking skill in one area (for instance considering the point of view of others), but be quite unable to transfer this skill to another area. It seems that the thinking skill remained embedded in the content. For this reason a few teachers are experimenting with the CoRT programme as a method for developing transferable thinking skills and also providing a cognitive 'core' to further directions for discussion.

General studies, liberal studies, humanities

Many schools have an open-ended subject area which is called by a variety of names. Often this is confined to the sixth form but sometimes it extends down through the school. The CoRT programme has fitted naturally into these areas: either in its own right or as a core to some discussion subject. The danger, of course, is that the content discussion may obscure the thinking processes.

English as a foreign language

Though this was never intended originally, the CoRT programme has been used very successfully as a basis for teaching English as a foreign language. Since language skill is developed by talking and thinking and understanding in that language, the CoRT programme provides the subject base. For many students it is more important to develop language skills associated with thinking about a subject or listening to someone else's thinking than skills associated with ordering a meal in a restaurant or reading literature in that language.

Head's contact lesson

This has been another unexpected use. Heads have used the CoRT programme as the basis for their contact lessons with the pupils.

They have felt that the lessons interfered with no one else's syllabus. The lessons require no special preparation or knowledge. They are easy to teach. The class develops into a sort of discussion session which allows the head to get to know the pupils and also to ascertain their feelings on a variety of subjects. In all respects, and by accident, the CoRT lessons seem ideal for this purpose. The disadvantage is that, though the lessons may serve the purpose of the head, the sporadic nature of the teaching makes them less useful for the purpose of teaching the different thinking skills.

For teaching practice

Some colleges of education are experimenting with the CoRT lessons as a subject for their students to teach when out on teaching practice. The suitability of the CoRT programme for this purpose is parallel to their suitability as a head's contact lesson (less interference with other school work and so on). In addition, the CoRT lessons provide a better opportunity to develop teaching skills – such as giving a sense of achievement – than most content-based subjects.

The above instances of the use of the CoRT programme are not recommendations, because that is not the purpose of this section. They represent the actual uses by schools of the material. As such the different placings of the subject illustrate both how schools have overcome the timetable problem and also how they see the subject. No doubt in most cases practical pressures have been considerably stronger than philosophical pressures. Furthermore the teacher who first showed interest in the subject, or the availability of a teacher who proved to be interested, must have strongly influenced the choice of place in which to try the new subject. Nevertheless all the uses seem reasonable and appropriate.

Placement considerations

As usual a number of dilemmas arise here. Is it better to have the subject tried in an inappropriate place or not at all? Is it better to have thinking treated as a separate subject or integrated into other subjects?

The advantage of treating thinking as a separate, specific subject in its own right is that it does then get full attention. The situation may be artificial and unnatural but it may be necessary to focus attention on the thinking processes themselves. Where the subject is used in another department, such as English, there is a considerable danger of its being swamped by the other subject. There is also the danger of so much adaptation (role-playing, content essays and so on) that the basic processes are lost sight of and do not get practised.

The disadvantage of treating CoRT as a separate subject is that what is learned may stay only within the confines of that subject.

I think it has less value to do the CoRT lessons on their own [instead of integrating them into other subjects] because they just become another lesson that doesn't have any relevance. You can't use CoRT as you can use biology. The children don't see any value in it and it is just 'something we do at school'.

This problem of transference will be treated later. It seems likely that CoRT processes are more readily transferred to areas outside school than to other school subjects, 'because the teacher won't know what I mean'.

The use of the CoRT programme as a core subject in integrated studies or interdisciplinary inquiry is an interesting one, because it may provide an opportunity for using the processes outside a pure 'thinking class'. The ideal situation would be to have some deliberate and focused practice on the thinking processes as such and then to use them in a variety of other areas, including other subjects such as geography or history.

At this stage it can be said that 'thinking as a subject' has been perceived by heads and teachers as being a fundamental subject rather than a speciality subject.

'The teaching of the processes by all teachers across a year with the aim of improving subjects and thinking is the "ideal" situation from my point of view, and that's what I shall aim at.'

Teacher training

At no point in the project has it been possible to set up formal teacher training, either at special centres or in the form of in-service courses. The most that any teacher received would have been a short lecture on the background theory, and even this would not have been available to more than a tiny percentage of those using the programme. Video-tapes of actual lessons as well as background theory are now becoming available, but so far teachers have had to rely entirely on the material contained in the programme itself, without any further aid or training.

This lack of training has not been a matter of choice but of necessity. In any case the rapid spread of the project would have made it impossible to provide training for all those involved. The lack of deliberate training fits in well with the evolutionary nature of the project: let teachers arrive at their own teaching style. There are, however, some obvious disadvantages:

Some teachers never feel confident enough to get started.

When difficulties are encountered a teacher may not know how to overcome them and may not realize that similar difficulties have been encountered by most teachers.

A teacher may set about teaching the material in a manner that is contrary to the learning method intended – for instance by focusing on content rather than on process; (this sort of problem will be discussed later).

A teacher's expectations may differ from the purposes of the programme, which may not be suited to his particular needs.

Inevitably there is a great deal of wastage: teachers who might have made a success of the course if they had received some training have given up. Nevertheless there are many who have succeeded without any specific training.

Use and experience

Thinking is not a complex subject unless one creates philosophical complexity for oneself. Certainly the CoRT lessons are very easy to understand. There is no complexity of structure, as there might be in any hierarchical subjects. For these reasons, training is not required to explain or teach the subject matter itself. Any teacher ought to be able to understand the material whatever his background. What is more difficult is the teaching method and style required in any open ended subject and in thinking in particular. In the absence of specific training it was suggested that teachers should acquire direct experience by using the material. They should feel their way through the course (or some section of it), developing their own method of teaching.

'They are just beginning to feel their way through. Mr F says that until he has gone through the whole thing himself he won't feel sure he's really getting his teeth into it. This means that it won't be until next year.'

'This year we are treating it as an experiment – mostly from the point of view of the teachers, who have to get to know it in the normal classroom situation.'

'So far I've kept it to myself because I want to work right through it first and I'm sure I'll do it much better next time.'

There are difficulties in this experience-through-use method. The biggest danger is that the first run through is treated as an experiment and not as the training process it should be. The awkwardness of the teacher as he acquires experience with the subject communicates itself to the pupils and the result is that the subject does not seem to work. It is impossible both to train the teacher and to try out the subject at the same time. The initial run through the course or part of it should be regarded solely as teacher training and teacher exploration. Once a teacher is familiar with the material and confident, then a proper trial of the subject can take place.

A lesser danger arises from the very rigid adherence to the teacher's booklet that seems necessary in the training period. Left on his own, with only the teacher's handbook, a teacher tends to follow the instructions very exactly. This means that he is reluctant to make the adaptations that are necessary for his own classroom or to introduce the topical variety that adds interest to the bare bones of the programme. This presents something of a dilemma, because if a teacher goes to the opposite extreme and neglects the handbook to teach entirely in his own way the first time round, he may end up teaching something quite different. Instances of this have occurred. It is probably better for the teacher to stick quite closely to the handbook the first time round and then use his own initiative rather more.

A particular difficulty arises with timing: the timing of the whole lesson and the timing of the individual practice items. The timing suggested in the teacher's handbook is very tight because it is intended for an experienced teacher working with a class of average ability. At first the teacher will probably require more time for each item or for the lesson. (If he cannot expand the lesson he picks fewer practice items.) As he acquires experience he tightens up the timing in order to keep to a brisk pace and to focus attention on the processes themselves, rather than on the content on which they are exercised. This point will be discussed further in a later section.

Teacher training

If it were possible to introduce deliberate teacher training then it should probably cover the following points:

Explanation of the purpose of each lesson and the most direct way of teaching the principle involved (avoiding confusion and philosophizing)

Training in the lead-in to the lessons with the use of topical examples and illustrations

Focus on the process/content dilemma and explanation of the danger of the lessons becoming discussion sessions or becoming content-based

The huge importance of the teacher's role in giving a sense of achievement in an open-ended subject

The need for a brisk pace and tight timing

Maintaining interest and the introduction of variety

Adaptation of the material for pupils of different ages and abilities

Setting the perspective of the whole subject and explaining the purpose to the pupils

The management of groups and group teaching in general

The different types of output (verbal, essay, notes and so on)

Integration of the CoRT processes into other subject areas and into thinking outside the classroom

Test procedures.

In the absence of formal training these are points to which a teacher ought to pay attention – using his own experience, judgement and initiative to provide some answers.

Teaching material

At this point a brief description of the actual teaching material used in the CoRT programme may be appropriate before discussing the teacher's reaction to it.

There are six sections, each of which consists of ten lessons. A section is designed to cover one term's work with one period a week. In practice this timetable is rarely adhered to, since some teachers find that they need more than one period a week whereas others find that in the experimental stage their teaching has to be somewhat sporadic. Each of the sections covers one general aspect of thinking:

I   (breadth)
II   (organization)
III   (interaction)
IV   (creativity)
V   (information and feeling)
VI   (action)

Within this general heading each lesson covers just one process, which is sometimes crystallized into a definite, if artificial, tool such as the PMI.

There is a teacher's handbook for each of the six sections. In addition, for each lesson there are lesson notes for each pupil.

Teacher's handbook

For most teachers the handbook is the only source of instruction or training. The handbook is different for each section but the basic features include:

Perspective, background and theory relating to the teaching of thinking in general and to the CoRT approach in particular

Teaching method, teaching points, difficulties and problems

Additional practice items for testing purposes and to supplement those provided in each lesson

Intention and purpose of each lesson

Teaching procedure and format for that section (although the general format is the same across the various sections the teaching format does vary from section to section)

Detailed teaching notes for each lesson in the section.

The material is quite tightly structured and the teaching notes are detailed. For instance the suggested practice time for each item is given and also the way in which it should be tackled (for instance group work, two to three minutes at the end of which the group spokesman gives the output; individual members of the group, or of other groups, can then add additional comments).

For many of the practice items 'suggested' answers are given. These are not meant to be the right answers, but they inevitably get treated us such by teachers. The reason for providing these suggestions is that in the middle of the lesson, with his mind on running the lesson, it may be difficult for the teacher to think of appropriate comments; the suggestions are provided as something to fall back on. Some teachers use these suggested answers as a way of giving a sense of achievement to pupils: 'Yes, you have given all the answers I have here in the handbook,' or: 'I have another answer down here; I wonder if you can get that one as well,' or: 'I think the answer you have given makes much more sense than the one given here,' or: 'What do you think of the suggestion given here? Do you agree with it?'

Most teachers seem to stick pretty closely to the handbook, at least the first time round. They often complain that the structure is too tight, that the practice items are unsuitable for certain ages or that the timing given is impractical. It is a curious phenomenon that those who wish to introduce variety or their own practice items feel inhibited from doing so by the presence of 'given' items. But most of the teachers seem to welcome the specific suggestions and the fact that the practice items are provided, instead of an exhortation to 'think of a problem and use it with the class'. As any teacher knows, it is very difficult to think of items for discussion, problem-solving or essay-writing if you have to do it on the spur of the moment, and if you have to provide some eight items per lesson. Such items must not require any special background knowledge and must provide the basis for thought and discussion. The difficulty in providing suitable practice items will be discussed in a later section. At this point it is noted that the detailed suggestions are provided for those who need them, and those who wish to introduce variety are free to do so – yet some teachers still complain about the detailed suggestions. It sometimes seems that this sort of complaint is not a practical 'user' complaint but a theoretical complaint directed at the material in an abstract sense.

The teacher's handbook also gives examples and illustrations with which to introduce each process. It is suggested, however, that the teacher should supplement these by local examples. Some teachers are very good at this and will turn any event to hand into an example.

Pupil's leaflets or pamphlets

Each pupil is provided with a leaflet that outlines the process that is the basis of the lesson and gives the items provided for practising that process. It was intended that the pupil should keep this leaflet for reference and revision and that by keeping it he would build up his own 'textbook' of thinking. In fact this rarely happens. The leaflets are given out at the beginning of the class and collected at the end for use in another class. This, of course, makes it impossible for the pupil to refer back to the lesson, and as a result the retention of the different processes is rather low. Composite review cards listing the various processes could possibly overcome this problem.

There is, however, a much more important point concerning the use of the leaflets. Clearly it is possible to teach the CoRT lessons without using the leaflets at all. The teacher could use the handbook and explain the basic process. He could then give the class practice items from his own single copy of the pupil's leaflet. There does not seem to be any need for the pupils to have a leaflet each. Indeed with the younger age groups it is claimed that giving out the leaflets is pointless, since in many cases their reading ability is too low to allow them to read through the leaflets. Others claim that the leaflets are essential to the lessons.

'Why do we need the leaflets?'

'The pupils who are less able readers get bogged down in the pamphlets. It varies according to the ability of the children.'

'The pamphlets are invaluable. It is something for them to have. It does make it more relevant for them and the pamphlets are used by the teacher to go step by step.'

'They found the pupils' leaflets very useful. I don't think the thing would have worked without the leaflets.

In fact although the leaflets are not *logically* necessary to the lesson they are *perceptually* necessary for the following reasons:

They make the lesson more definite, more concrete and more serious instead of seeming to be something dreamed up by the teacher for that class

Thinking is a pretty nebulous subject and needs anchoring with some focus of attention

In the case of CoRT II, CoRT IV and CoRT V the cover design on the leaflet actually illustrates the process that is to be taught in the lesson and can be used to introduce the lesson

Although a pupil can understand what a teacher says he has no way of knowing *what the teacher is going to say next*; with the leaflets he has it all in front of him and can see the basic nature of the lesson and its extent

The leaflets allow the teacher to go through the lesson step by step

The leaflets provide a visual identity for each lesson and, perhaps, a retainable visual image.

As at so many other points in the discussion of the teaching of thinking one is faced with a situation in which it is *possible* to do something in one way but much less effective than doing it another way. It is possible to teach the lesson without any pupil leaflets, but it seems to be less effective and the pupils tend to get bored more quickly. They also complain, not surprisingly, that the lessons all seem the same (lack of visual distinction).

Teachers who prefer to ease the pupils into the lesson with a lot of examples and much discussion do not like using the leaflets because they 'give the game away'. Such teachers prefer to maintain the inductive approach, in which pupils practise the process without ever being aware that they are doing so until the teacher tells them at the end of the lesson. This approach may suit the teaching of other subjects (discovery method), but it does not suit the teaching of thinking, which is based more on self-conscious practice than on discovery – since there is nothing to discover. Nevertheless an inductive approach right at the beginning of the lesson is very useful, and the leaflets can be given out after the point has been drawn from the example and crystallized into the process that is to be the subject of the lesson.

The CoRT Thinking lesson

The underlying structure of each lesson is very simple. A basic process is to be the subject of attention during that lesson. There are practice items on which to practise the process. To some extent the simplicity of the lesson is a disadvantage. It seems to provide an invitation to over-elaborate, over-complicate and over-philosophize. This is understandable because there is not much you can do with a simple process except to state it, and that is not very interesting.

The process

The process is something to do or something to look at. The distinction between the two is not clear cut. All the processes are attention-directors of one sort or another, as discussed in the first half of this book. The OPV from CoRT I requires the student to look deliberately at the views of the other people involved in the situation. The 'focus' lesson from CoRT II encourages the habit of pausing in the course of thinking in order to determine exactly what is being considered at the moment. The 'Being Wrong' lesson from CoRT III looks at two of the main sources of error in thinking: exaggeration and false generalizations and the habit of arguing from only part of the situation. The random-input lesson from CoRT IV (creativity) practises the process of using a random word to trigger off new ideas. The 'values' lesson from CoRT V suggests the division of values into high and low in order to encourage a closer examination of the values involved in a situation. The 'operations' lesson from CoRT VI focuses on the deliberate setting out of action steps.

In some lessons the process involves looking in a direction and then 'listing' what one sees. In other lessons it is a matter of looking in order to pick out some pattern. In yet others the operation may consist of asking a certain question and then finding the answer to it.

The process is explained with illustrations and examples. It is left to the teacher to provide the overall framework which shows the relevance of the process to the whole thinking process. This may be a weakness of the material.

Practice items

These are designed for practising the process outlined above. The items may be short and may require no more than an answer to a question or a simple discrimination. In other cases it may be a matter of picking things out or putting them in order. Most of the practice items, however, are in the form of problems or proposals. The pupils are asked to consider the situation presented and then to apply the process that is being practised. There are no definite right or wrong answers.

A number of different practice items are given and in most lessons the teacher can choose those items which he feels are most suitable for his class.

A rapid run through a number of different practice items is recommended in order to keep attention on the process. This creates great problems in terms of drift into content and the maintenance of interest. These problems will be considered later.

The choice of practice items and their nature also creates problems, because pupils are apt to prefer those problems about which they normally do little thinking.

Simple but different

Although the structure of the lessons could not be simpler, difficulty arises because the lessons are *different* from other lessons. It is not a matter of learning something but of *practising* something. Once attention has been focused as required it all seems easy and obvious. Teaching the obvious is not easy.

Teaching points

In the teaching of thinking as a subject some important points must be made about the teaching method. The main points are discussed below. In many cases the teaching points are also teaching problems arising from the subject itself or from the particular CoRT approach. Later in this book there is a specific section on these problems, but in some cases this section and the problem section will overlap, since a teaching point can become a teaching problem if it is difficult to carry out.

Puzzlement

'They found CoRT a bit puzzling at first. They didn't quite know what they were doing, what it was all about. That is a case of conditioning. They expect a certain sort of lesson and if they can't see the immediate usefulness of the work they wonder.'

'They didn't know what it was all about. They must see the immediate consequences of what they are about. They wondered whether they were going to be assessed or questioned on it.'

'There was slow progress at first. The pupils found it so alien and outside normal teaching that it "threw them".'

'I think they just enjoy talking and they accepted that they were having lessons on "thinking" just as they had had SRA and "learning to read". They thought it was called "Learning to think".'

This puzzlement would arise with any new curriculum subject.

It probably arises more with thinking than with any other subject because both teachers and pupils feel self-conscious and bashful about the idea of learning to think. In fact the thinking lessons are very rarely referred to as such and are usually called by the neutral name of 'CoRT', standing by itself. There is additional puzzlement for the children, in that they are allowed to talk and think, and encouraged to do so. This is in sharp contrast with other lessons. One child was amazed to find that he 'could sit and think'. The lack of a knowledge content, a learning process, and a hierarchical structure adds to the bewilderment. As suggested in the preceding section, it is the simplicity of the lessons that is so puzzling.

This situation involves two important teaching points. The first is that the teacher should be confident. He should push ahead with the lesson in a definite rather than a tentative manner. A teacher's puzzlement only compounds the pupils' puzzlement. It is better for the teacher to be confident and wrong than hesitant and right. The second point is that the teacher should try and put the lessons in some sort of perspective. He should explain the purpose of practising thinking skills. He should explain the value of being able to discuss and think of things outside the knowledge syllabus. Suggestions about this are given in the teacher's handbook but, above all, those reasons which seem valid to the teacher himself are the ones that he should use.

With younger children there is less of a problem because they accept things more easily and the curriculum in the primary school is more fluid. The problem is worst with the older, subject-bound and examination-orientated pupils.

Discussion, content and process

This is one of the two most important (and difficult) teaching points. The other is 'achievement'. The lessons are discussion lessons in so far as what goes on in the lessons is discussion among groups of pupils or between pupils and teacher. From moment to

moment that is what is usually happening. The explaining part of
the lesson is quite short because each process is easy to explain.
The pupils enjoy discussion:

'I sometimes just have to keep quiet. It just interrupts the train
of thought, it's quite unusual – for several minutes I feel
superfluous in the classroom. They don't want me in it, they
resent interruption.'

Yet the purpose of the lessons is *not* to provide open-ended, free-
flowing discussion sessions but to practise deliberately some
specific thinking processes. Discussion, therefore, has to be cur-
tailed and disciplined:

'Without a firm focal point class tutor periods often develop into
open-ended discussion periods with a few lively pupils expressing
their point of view while the rest of the class sit silent and passive.
CoRT Thinking provides a disciplined enough format to avoid
such unproductive gossip sessions, while at the same time its subjects for discussion are flexible and wide enough to include the
whole class.'

'The children work ever so well. They love discussing. Discussions are now disciplined by using the CoRT framework.'

'They need this tight time limit – it prevents it degenerating
into a general chat. In schools they tend to have too much
waffling on.'

The purpose of the 'disciplined' discussion and the 'tight' time
limits is not to improve discussion as such but to shift the pupils
from one problem to another, so that their attention stays on the
thinking process that is being practised. It must be said that this is
not an easy teaching matter. The pupils love to get their teeth
into one particular problem and to discuss it at length. They do
find it difficult to shift their attention to a completely different
problem – seemingly at the whim of the teacher. They do not see
as clearly as the teacher the 'practice' purpose of the lesson – it
just seems to them that they are being cut short when they have a
lot more to say on the issue.

If it is difficult for the pupils, it seems to be just as difficult for
the teachers. Many teachers are so delighted to find the pupils
becoming interested in anything that they let the discussion proceed and even encourage it to do so. They feel that if the pupils are

vigorously discussing something then this represents good education. They also feel that if the pupils are thinking that is also good thinking practice. So a whole lesson may be devoted to the subject of 'smoking' when in fact this is only one practice item for which the pupils are supposed to give the point of view of a father and of his thirteen-year-old daughter who wishes to smoke (OPV lesson in CoRT I). The situation is complicated by the fact that some teachers (especially when the lessons are used as heads' contact lessons) use the lessons as an oblique opportunity to discuss important things such as careers, discipline, smoking and so on.

It is easy enough for me to write that a balance ought to be kept between the purpose of the lesson as a thinking lesson and the value of the discussion. But in practice it is much more difficult for the teacher in the classroom to achieve that 'balance'. As in so much teaching, there are no hard and fast rules. It may be enough for the teacher to keep firmly in mind the following two points:

The purpose of the lesson is to practise specific thinking processes and the way of keeping attention on the processes is to use a number of different practice items.

A general discussion might be very interesting and involving and yet leave no transferable thinking skill behind.

Another problem arises with 'red herrings'. A boy who has never said much at any time in any class suddenly comes out with an idea which is only remotely connected to the discussion. Does the teacher rule it out as irrelevant and so shut the boy up, or does he welcome this opportunity of bringing the boy into discussion and giving him confidence?

'This was the first time Johnny had spoken. It started a discussion that lasted most of the lesson. I think it did him a lot of good.'

As far as the thinking lesson was concerned, and perhaps even as far as the other pupils were concerned, the Johnny discussion might have been a complete waste of time. As a principle it is not possible to follow up all red herrings, even though they seem promising as discussion points. In exceptional cases the needs of a particular pupil may override these other considerations. But it must be kept firmly in mind that discussion for discussion's sake is not the purpose of the lessons.

Use of terminology

The discussion nature of the lessons makes it difficult to keep attention on the process. What tends to happen is that the teacher introduces the process at the beginning of the lesson and probably uses the artificial CoRT terminology at this point. For the rest of the lesson it is *taken for granted* that the lesson is about that process and the terminology is never used again. For example in the PMI lesson the teacher will explain what PMI stands for and then say that it really means looking for the good and bad points. For the rest of the lesson he will ask the pupils to give the good and bad points and never again mention the PMI. Teachers are diffident about using strange and seemingly unnecessary terminology: 'If you can ask for the good and bad points why do we need a PMI?' The code 'PMI' was created specifically as an attention-focusing device. If at each stage in the lesson the teacher asks for a PMI then this becomes a shorthand instruction which sticks in the pupils' minds and which they themselves can use on future occasions. Similarly in the OPV lesson the teacher will ask the pupils to 'give the viewpoints of the other people' rather than to 'do an OPV'.

The difficulty pupils have in remembering or distinguishing the different processes (discussed later in the problem section) arises directly from this diffidence on the part of the teachers, who do not realize that to practise a process is not the same as *consciously* to practise a process.

At all stages, and beyond the needs of the moment, the teacher should attempt to repeat the process and talk in terms of the process. This is the only way of keeping some attention on the process itself as distinct from the discussion.

Teaching from the centre outwards

Teaching from the boundary inwards is the more usual teaching method. At the boundary we learn to distinguish one thing from another. Then we group together all those things which we have distinguished from other things. We abstract the important principles and we now have a definition or a class of objects. Induction works in the same way. So does the discovery method. So does the traditional method of teaching thinking by abstraction and generalization.

But with CoRT one teaches from the centre outwards. The thinking processes are artificially carved out and crystallized – it is not a matter of discovery but of use. The teacher illustrates the process with very clear-cut examples and avoids boundary examples. The reason for this is that there is a deliberate overlap in the CoRT processes, since they are intended to be practical processes, not philosophical distinctions. Unless the teacher teaches from the centre outwards the pupils are apt to become confused.

For example a pupil may ask about the difference between doing an OPV (other people's viewpoint) and an EBS (examine both sides of the argument). It may seem that in both cases one is looking at someone else's viewpoint. In practice OPV is used to consider the views of all the people in a situation involving decision or planning (moving house, increasing prices, changing school and so on), whereas EBS is used specifically in relation to an argument. In the EBS procedure the person actually takes over the other side of the argument and tries to develop it – even beyond the actual view of the other person. Obviously in some cases OPV and EBS overlap and the teacher should not be afraid of saying so. The important thing is that the examples should be clear and definite in order to illustrate the *practical* use of the process, not its philosophical distinction from other processes.

'I have found a considerable overlap. This doesn't bother the pupils but it tends to bother me. This may be because I worked in scholastic philosophy.'

A surprising number of teachers have this problem, which may arise from the important role played by 'distinguish . . .' and 'why is this different from . . .?' in ordinary teaching.

The AGO lesson has always caused problems because the teacher tries to make a distinction between aims, goals and objectives: 'Aims, goals and objectives. I had some difficulty myself in distinguishing between an aim, a goal and an objective.'

Once the difficulty was appreciated it was pointed out in the handbook that they should all be treated as the same, with the explanation that in some cases it was more usual to use one or other term. This has not really solved the problem, because once the three words are used in the lesson heading people seem to feel an *appetite* to make distinctions, even beyond what is required.

At this point the danger of philosophizing should be mentioned. The teacher and, sometimes, the pupils indulge in subtle distinctions and qualifications instead of regarding the CoRT processes as rough tools designed for practical use: 'He is a first class teacher – quick and lively *but* I had one or two reservations as to the abstractions he was trying to get across in the AGO lesson.'

In this particular case the practice item had suggested that the pupils might have won a large sum of money on the football pools and they were asked to give their 'aims' in spending the money. One pupil replied that he would buy a big car. The teacher pointed out that this was not his real aim (which was to enjoy himself or to show off), but only a means of carrying through his real aim. A distinction was being made between the real aim and the means of carrying it out. The problem is a valid one for this example, and it could be tackled in terms of general aims and particular aims; or in terms of ultimate aims and immediate aims and so on. These sorts of problem do arise quite often. It is better, however, for the teacher to tackle them in a practical manner (for example, 'they are all aims') rather than build a philosophical edifice which may apply only to particular problems.

The danger of confusion is always much greater than the danger of philosophical inexactitude.

Explaining the process

The teacher has to start the lesson at some point. He could say: 'Today we are going to look at the process of guessing.' He would then proceed to explain what it was about, with the aid of the cover on the pupils' notes and the material in them. After some discussion with the class the practice items could be tackled.

Alternatively the teacher could lead 'inductively' into the lesson by using a topical example:

'What do you think I have in this box on the desk?'

'Do you think it is going to be a good summer?'

He might draw a distinction between knowledge and guessing:

'Do you know where you are going on holiday?'

'Do you know what will happen to you?'

Or he might even tell a story (perhaps from the newspaper or television) of the man who did not realize he was guessing when he made an important decision.

In a to-and-fro discussion with the class, the teacher might draw out the principle of guessing. This would then be crystallized quite rapidly into the form used in the CoRT lesson. The crystallized process would be illustrated with the examples given in the pupils' notes. Some further examples would be given by the pupils. The practice items would then be tackled. Throughout the lesson the teacher himself would keep clearly in mind that the CoRT structure of the lesson was only a device to get pupils into the habit of examining their guesses.

In the way the lessons are introduced, in the way the processes are explained and in the way the emphasis is placed, there are considerable differences from teacher to teacher.

'One teacher found a way she called the "pin man" [CAF lesson]. In this she drew on the board a problem with a big ring round it and encouraged the pupils to think about walking round the problem looking in from different points of view, and then walking into the middle of the problem and looking out in different directions. She said they seemed able to do this, although it was only an image and not a method. It was something concrete which they could think of doing – looking at all points and walking round.'

Topicality can be introduced only by the teacher: 'This lesson went particularly well as the students are at present upset about a particular new rule and we could discuss this.'

Achievement

Any lesson should be an environment so structured that the pupils can genuinely earn praise. A sense of achievement is vital to any education process, or indeed to behaviour in general. Achievement is a complex and subtle thing: the achievement of working out a jigsaw puzzle or crossword puzzle; the achievement of an improved golf round; the achievement of winning at tennis; the achievement of capturing a likeness in a drawing; the achievement of successful gardening. Sometimes it is a matter of knowing where one wants to go and getting there – as in mountain climbing. Sometimes it is a matter of feeling that you are doing something well – as in skiing. Sometimes it is a matter of someone else telling you that you are doing well – as in drama.

If you can see the objective clearly, you know when you have reached it. If there is a finite measure of improvement, you may know that you have improved. If there are right answers or definite items of information, then you know that you have found them. If things work out, as in solving a problem, you also know that you have achieved something. Unfortunately almost all these things are absent in an open-ended subject which is not content-based.

With CoRT lessons there are no 'right' answers. Nor is there any fixed knowledge against which to check one's memory or understanding. Improvement can be judged only by an outsider. For all these reasons it is entirely up to the teacher to give the pupils a sense of achievement in the CoRT lessons.

The teacher gives a sense of achievement in a number of different ways.

Listening

It is essential that the teacher should listen to each of the ideas or suggestions that are offered. Similarly when younger children are asked to make drawings it is essential that the teacher should collect them all up (even if she never has a chance to examine each one). The mere fact that the teacher listens and pays attention to something is a form of achievement for the pupil.

Response

In the CoRT lessons the teacher has to develop an extensive repertoire of responses that give a sense of value in the absence of definite right or wrong answers.

> That's very interesting.
> That's the most unusual idea I have heard.
> That's a very original idea.
> That idea links up with Joe's but takes it a bit further.
> That sounds interesting; could you explain it further?
> A very important point.
> An obvious point but one that could easily be overlooked.
> I hadn't thought of that.
> That's a nice idea.

This repertoire of responses is elaborated further in the CoRT teacher's handbook. The basic idea is to let each pupil know that his or her idea has some special value. It may not be the most important idea but it may be original or interesting. There is the usual danger that with his responses a teacher may be shaping the thinking of the pupils by guiding them towards the types of idea he seems to prefer. The importance of giving a sense of achievement, however, overrides this danger.

Marks

In the pilot stages of the CoRT programme a marking system was devised whereby the other pupils could assess the value of an idea that had been put forward, and also compare their assessment with that of the teacher (with a bonus for matching). This worked very well in some schools and encouraged the competitive spirit. On the whole, however, it seemed cumbersome, artificial and open to abuse. The possibility of devising a better marking system is not excluded, but with an open-ended subject like thinking it is probably not appropriate. A simpler 'credit' system, with a few rewards for really excellent ideas, remains to be explored.

Teacher's handbook

As suggested in a previous section, some teachers use the suggestions given in the handbook as a basis of comparison for the pupils: 'I reward the children by saying: "You have already got five of the six ideas put forward in this handbook".' The handbook answers are not treated as absolute and the teacher can praise a pupil for an idea that is better than the one given in the handbook, or for an important idea that has been left out of the handbook.

Blackboard

If a teacher writes on the blackboard a list of the ideas put forward, then a pupil, or group, who adds another idea gets a sense of achievement from seeing it added to the list. This 'concretization' of achievement is important. The same effect can be achieved by the teacher asking: 'Which group has more than five points on this item?'

In general the ability to add a new point gives a strong sense of achievement. But there is a danger. A group that has worked very hard but has managed to produce only ideas that have already been put forward by the other groups may get no sense of achievement at all if the emphasis is entirely on adding to the general list. For the same reason it may create problems about which group is asked first for its ideas, since the starting group will get all its ideas down and the last group may get none at all. A simple solution is to go round and collect one idea at a time from each group. Another solution is to ask for written lists of ideas so that there is a record of each group's achievement.

'They depended for their sense of achievement on whether the teacher took their idea and put it on the board.'

Tests

In theory it would be possible to give the pupils a sense of achievement by testing them before and after CoRT lessons and showing the improvement. It could also be done by comparing their work with that of a group who had not done any CoRT lessons. The differences are often great, yet they are not convincing because a pupil will feel that he would have done better anyway. It is very difficult for a pupil to accept that his thinking has improved because the improvement is imperceptible to him, and also because it implies that his thinking was not perfect before.

In general it must said that giving a sense of achievement in any open-ended subject, and in CoRT lessons in particular, is difficult. Whatever strategy is adopted it must depend in the end on the teacher: 'In the end the subjects get their sense of achievement from the teacher. They get it from the way I react.'

This creates problems where the teacher has not established a definite role with regard to the pupils. With younger children who are still anxious to please the teacher it is rather easier than with older children, who may regard the teacher only as a source of knowledge.

Control and discipline

'Discipline was good, but at first they equated no writing with no work and there were problems. But the fact of their all having the leaflets "pinned it down". They could use the processes in English.'

In contrast to some other subject areas the teacher cannot control the class from the position of authority as holder of 'the book of knowledge'. He cannot control the class through being the possessor of unlimited critical power (as in English). The ideas turned up by the pupils may be as good as those of the teacher or better – and the pupils can see this for themselves. There are no arbitrary rules which the teacher can hold up his sleeve and suddenly reveal.

In the thinking lessons control is a matter of leadership. Control must be by initiative. The teacher must maintain a brisk pace. The teacher decides which problem to tackle and when to stop and move on to the next thing. The teacher decides which group or pupil he is going to ask for an answer.

'This is also useful because it creates almost a total discussion process, and one of the good things is that you must keep up the brisk pace of the lesson. If you keep up the brisk pace you have far fewer problems.'

'I like to stop them before they have finished a discussion.'

In this sort of situation the teacher should never be in a position where he has to plead with the pupils for their approval or co-operation.

Discipline depends on interest. If the teacher finds that interest is slipping away, then he should introduce variety and may, for the moment, concentrate more on the content interest than on the practice of the process itself. All these points are matters of general teaching technique and as such are not peculiar to the CoRT lessons, or even to teaching thinking, except that the problem may be accentuated by the open-ended nature of the subject.

Comments

The following comments from a research worker who observed a CoRT lesson in progress indicate the sort of thing that can go wrong:

The groups were never properly formed. Some children had private conversations. Some didn't know what to do, some did nothing at all.

The points weren't really collected from each group.

The teacher made more points than the pupils, so they followed her thinking. She never collected or followed theirs. Her questions were too specific, leading too much towards a particular response.

The pupils' responses were slight and hesitant at first and only became more confident when the teacher's questions became more specific.

The teacher rewarded with 'That's right' if she approved of the idea and with a question if she did not.

The teacher never carried out the basic process herself. She didn't do an 'immediate' C & S herself.

Mechanics of
the thinking lessons

Group work

'I prefer working with others in a group rather than on my own.'

'In groups you have different views. You can get caught on one track, and another person might have a different track.'

'I don't use whole class discussion because there are over thirty of them, and they inhibit each other, and if they are interested they all want to say something together.'

'During the CoRT lesson the pupils were working in informal groupings and the interchange between the sexes was equal and openly friendly. The visitor, an experienced teacher, said he had never seen such a naturally co-operative effort between girls and boys before.'

'A useful bonus in using the course comes as a result of its small-group format. Sooner or later even the most diffident child has a turn at being spokesman for the group and because he is expressing ideas the group has fed him – and not necessarily having to take any initiative other than actually summarizing the group's points – he has a shield of non-personal commitment between himself and the teacher. This has helped several quieter children in my class to vocalize in public much more easily. Since there are no right or wrong answers in these lessons a climate of confidence is produced.'

'Group work makes the pupils think longer, thus giving those who are not so quick a chance to have and express ideas.'

'Groups are always eager to be the first to answer – that's my problem!'

'The great advantage of group work is that you get far more involved once you have eight kids and six arguments going on at the same time.'

The dynamics and advantages of group work are not peculiar to the teaching of thinking. But group work is an important part of the CoRT approach. Some schools have been quite used to group work, but in many schools the use of group work in the thinking lessons has provided the only point in the curriculum for it. The advantages of group work in the teaching of thinking are as follows:

In an open class the teacher's questions are invariably answered by the same bright pupils and the others take no part in the thinking process. With the class divided into groups, less bright pupils have a chance to contribute, or at least to watch in action the thinking of the others.

Where there are five groups there is five times as much discussion going on in a class as there would have been without any groups.

Shy pupils and pupils who are worried about their ideas being 'right' can operate with more confidence in a group.

In a group pupils are forced to listen to the ideas of others because in turn they want their own ideas to be listened to.

A peer group is a more natural thinking situation than a teacher-pupil relationship.

Since groups work independently, at the end there is a greater variety of ideas than if the teacher had asked for individual responses in an open class (where one person's views would have influenced everyone else).

The groups allow 'thinking time'. It would be difficult for a teacher to say to a class: 'I want all of you to sit and think about this for three minutes,' but with groups as much thinking time as is needed can be allowed, since it is really discussion time.

The groups have a spokesman, who gives the group's output at the end of the allowed time. There may be a separate note-taker who takes down the ideas and summarizes them, or the spokesman may do this as well. On the whole the group format works very well but there are some disadvantages:

'In my group it is definitely becoming a business where you have one or two in each group who do it. They have a discussion of sorts, but I think, watching them, that it is the half-dozen in the class who are doing the lessons and the others are following on.' 'Now funnily enough in my group it is totally different. I get a better response right across the board.'

'One of the difficulties of working in a group is that the group may reject an idea from an individual when that idea would really be acceptable.'

'In a group it never did work well. You tend to rely on one or two to give the ideas. You can see that two or three or more of the group are dozing off. I can keep my eye on the whole class and make sure they are all contributing to the lesson, or you know the ones who aren't likely to contribute anyway and you can draw them in. But in a group where they are given two or three minutes to work on it, I have to go round and chivvy the group and eventually they will write something down. You can talk to the other teachers. It appears they're doing this more and more.'

'A disadvantage of group work is that it sometimes gets dominated by one pupil.'

'The high-achieving pupils don't like group work because they say they can't show the rest of the class how good their idea is since it is lost in the group output. They feel they don't get the recognition they deserve.'

Picking groups

The teacher may pick the groups at random or he may try to arrange them so that each group has a mixture of bright talkative children and others who are more reticent. He may also try to put all the clowns and trouble-makers into one group so that they neutralize each other rather than disrupting every group. Once the groups are formed the teacher may want to move pupils around if he finds that one person is dominating a group too much – or disturbing it.

The pupils may also be allowed to form their own groups:

'They don't work so well in friendship groups as they chat about everything but the lesson. So you have to split them up.'

'I pick out five good sensible children and then I let them pick their groups, one at a time.'

'The group structure seems to have worked well because they do work and stick together as a group. In fact they still go on using the same group structure in the other part of the lesson, that is the family part.'

When the groups have been formed they are usually kept for a term or changed once during a term.

With mixed-ability classes there would seem to be a choice between mixed-ability groups, with the less able scattered throughout them, or groups based on ability. There is insufficient evidence to favour either approach. When groups are based on ability there is less chance of the brighter members of a group completely dominating the others. Furthermore the teacher can always make a point of asking the less able group to give their output first. It is also possible to let the less able groups go on working on one problem when the more able groups have already moved on to the next problem. In such cases the teacher would sit in with the group to hear their output.

With remedial classes the class should be small enough to function as a single group. The teacher then sits in with the group during the discussion but must not attempt to guide it.

Group size varies from four to eight. This depends on the size of the class and the articulateness of the pupils. There should not be too many separate groups in a class because getting the output from each group would then take a long time. On the other hand a large group of articulate children nearly always splits into two groups for discussion.

Individual work

Although the CoRT lessons are primarily group based there are a number of situations in which pupils work and respond as individuals:

in the introduction to each lesson and in general discussions about points that arise and about the 'process' that is the subject of the lesson

where, although the pupils may work as a group, the teacher is still able to ask questions of individuals; similarly an individual may add a further point of his own to the output of his group or another group

where the teacher prefers to work with the whole class or a class of very able pupils prefer to work as individuals

where the output is written, for instance an essay; this may occur during the lesson itself or take the form of project work to be done between lessons

several items in the CoRT lessons are short items which work better on an open-class basis since there is no need for discussion; such practice items are usually designated as open-class items in the teacher's notes for that lesson:

In general the basic work is group work with an admixture of open-class work.

Output

The output is usually oral. Group spokesmen or individuals give their ideas and the teacher responds. Sometimes the teacher may write down the ideas on the blackboard. The oral output seems to have a lot of advantages, quite apart from the fact that it is much quicker and the rest of the class can hear what is being said. The thinking of many pupils is restricted when it has to be expressed in writing. Furthermore pupils tend to adopt a formal 'written' approach when asked to express their views in writing.

'They are a splendid lot, talkative, lively, interested. Their ability and confidence are very poorly expressed in their written work.'

'Writing was inhibiting. They became individuals again. They became concerned with how they were writing and what they were writing. And once they were writing their own notes they became introspective, separated themselves from the group and sat there as individuals all writing their own ideas and not generating ideas in the group.'

'In the CoRT lessons they are not handicapped by having to express things in writing.'

'They had used exercise books for project work but this was dropped a) because their English needed too much correction and b) because they liked group discussion but were less interested when it was a matter of writing. So I normally say: "Why don't you have a little chat amongst yourselves in your groups?" They get one person to write down their ideas and then we discuss them.'

In an oral output the teacher can pursue a matter further or ask for an elaboration. The quality of expression may not matter as much as the content although in an English lesson one would expect some attention to be paid to this aspect as well.

The exact method for collecting the groups' outputs is discussed in the teacher's handbook, since it can vary from lesson to lesson. For instance in some cases one group gives its whole output and then other groups are invited to add new points only. In other cases each group provides one point at a time in rotation. Sometimes one group works on one aspect of the problem and another group works on another aspect.

From time to time written outputs may be used. Younger children often clamour to put something down in writing because they feel they are not really doing any 'work' unless some writing is involved. Very able pupils also prefer to put things down in writing because they like to have time to organize their thoughts in the best possible way, instead of just spilling them out. The slower and more careful thinkers sometimes feel they are at a disadvantage if they have to express their thoughts aloud. Project work is written. Tests are written. In addition the teacher may ask for written output during the lesson itself on a practice item. This is usually done only with the more able groups, as the less able take too long to get going. There does seem to be more of an air of 'seriousness' and achievement when written output is requested.

Written output can take various forms. The most obvious is the essay. The essay is not, however, always suitable, since it tends to argue a case and the construction may be too laboured. Sometimes it is better to have the output in list form ('List your priorities in this situation') or in note form. The advantage of lists or notes is that the teacher has an easier task when it comes to separating, sorting and assessing the ideas. From the pupils' point of view, attention is shifted from the business of connecting up ideas to the ideas themselves. (The consequences of an action are dealt with just as well in note form as in essay form.) A further form of output could be called 'box-filling'. Here the teacher sets out the boxes or headings and the pupils have to put something under each heading ('Put something in the P box, and M box and the I box'). This is suitable for younger children.

Drama, role-playing and drawing are other possible types of output and have been explored by teachers. Some of the CoRT lessons lend themselves well to role-playing. These variations can add interest, provided they do not take over so completely that the basic purpose of the lesson is lost.

Problems

Most things can be regarded as problems. Some of the 'problems' encountered in the practical attempt to teach thinking directly as a curriculum subject have been described in preceding sections. These problems are mentioned again briefly here, and some new basic problems are dealt with in greater detail.

Problems discussed elsewhere

PROBLEM REGARDING TIMETABLE

Finding a place to put the CoRT lessons. Deciding whether to run the lessons on their own or to put them into some existing subject. Choosing that subject area.

PROBLEM REGARDING INVOLVEMENT AND INTENTION

Making a serious attempt to try out the subject. Finding a teacher interested enough to get involved. The danger of 'dabbling'.

PROBLEM OF EXPECTATIONS

Both teacher and pupil may have expectations that are too high, or are unrelated to the actual material. Disappointment if the expectations are not fulfilled. (Common to all new curriculum projects.)

PROBLEM OF PUZZLEMENT

Pupils find this open-ended subject different from other subjects and are not quite sure what to make of it or how to treat it. The need for perspective. Teacher and pupils need 'to develop a frame of mind about the work'.

PROBLEM OF TEACHER-TRAINING

Perhaps not a problem in as much as many teachers find that the material, plus their own initial experience, is enough. Nevertheless there is probably a high wastage of teachers who would have been more successful had there been some basic training.

PROBLEM OF TEACHING PROCESS, NOT CONTENT

The very important and difficult problem of keeping attention on the thinking process that is the subject of the lesson, and not allowing attention to be captured by discussion of content. The problem of changing practice items when the pupils prefer to treat one of them in depth.

PROBLEM OF ACHIEVEMENT

Common to all open-ended subjects. How to give a sense of achievement when there are no 'right' answers and no definite items of information. The importance of the teacher's role and the problem of teaching style.

PROBLEM OF TERMINOLOGY

This problem will be dealt with later in this section.

PROBLEM OF PHILOSOPHIZING

The tendency of some teachers to over-complicate matters and to confuse the pupils by treating the CoRT processes as philosophical analyses rather than as practical tools with deliberate overlap.

Problem of sameness

This is an important problem because it is mentioned again **and** again.

'Although each of the items is different, the pattern is **very** much the same in each lesson. At first there is a comfort in this in that they know what's going to happen. But after ten or so lessons they can become repetitive. That's why I think it's a good thing after ten or so lessons to have a piece of work into which you introduce these processes where relevant.'

'What they found difficult to grasp was the difference between certain thinking processes, and some expressed the opinion that these divisions were artificial. They found AGO particularly difficult.'

'I wonder if they would have found it – no, tedious is not the right word – if I'd done it every week? You can always tell with pupils, for the standard of work falls when they start getting bored.'

'In fact in talking with the pupils afterwards and in looking at their written work, I found that they had distinguished only between PMI and the rest and some denied that they could even do that. "They're all just the same," one boy said, and the rest agreed. "You just make a list".'

'It can become repetitive after ten lessons, going through the practical side of the process. That's why I think it wise to introduce something else, to introduce them to a piece of work.'

'I'm trying to avoid the difficulty of each lesson seeming the same – so I spend time crystallizing the process.'

Pupil: 'I thought they were the same sort of thing. All the lessons are very much related.'

'Certainly at one time I did four in a row and by the time the fourth one had come there was a certain staleness.'

Pupil: 'I just combine all the lessons. I can't think of any one individually. I think they are all the same sort of thing. The PMI, the first one we did ... In fact when I came to the second week I thought we did it all the first week, so what can we do now? I think they are all very much related.'

'I am quite interested in not teaching it the way the handbook says – which I have been doing with one lesson on each of the processes. Because if you have pupils practising dribbling or heading *every* lesson and never playing a game of football, then they get very bored. I taught CoRT I and II and we all [the other teachers] felt that it was hard work just to keep going on the skills and processes. I am interested in working out a way of teaching a topic and introducing these processes to make sure that we do them properly and that we relate them to something relevant. It is all right doing "yellow cars" but when they've done these empty thinking processes every week . . . they should be made to relate it to their other subjects.'

The problem is an important one and it is made more difficult by the fact that it is circular. Teachers play down the processes in order to generate content interest, and as a result the lessons seem all the same. It is undoubtedly true that each lesson is a 'thinking' lesson. If the teacher is happy for the lesson to proceed as a dis- cussion lesson with little attempt to focus on the process, then each lesson will indeed be the same sort of discussion lesson.

The whole purpose of the artificial terminology is to create different areas of attention. If these are ignored by the teacher, who feels it is enough that the pupils are having an interesting discussion, then the purpose of the differentiation is defeated. Each lesson then becomes a matter of 'discuss this' and 'discuss this next'. The distinction of the lessons can be maintained only if the teacher focuses very firmly on the purpose of each lesson and em- phasizes the process. He must make it clear that what he wants from each group is an attempt to apply the process – not just the results of general discussion. The problem is that the pupils will not confine themselves to the process, but will have a general discussion anyway. By crystallizing the process, by showing its practical application, by repeating the purpose of the lesson and by using the terminology, the teacher can reduce this problem of sameness.

To some extent the problem is created by the teacher. This is not entirely so, because some pupils may be unable to see the difference between processes even when the teacher has tried to demonstrate it.

The lessons are only a framework and it is necessary for the teacher to introduce variety by introducing specific pieces of work or projects from time to time (say every fourth lesson). He should also attempt to use the processes in other areas. Changes in the format of the lessons, such as role-playing, are to be encouraged.

At first teachers are hesitant to do this because they try to follow the handbook quite closely until they have become familiar with the new subject. The second time round they feel freer to experiment and innovate. Almost all the quotations used above were from first-time teachers.

Certainly the problem is one that needs recognizing. The solution is twofold:

Emphasize the processes and the distinct purpose of each lesson; do not be content with a general discussion each time.

Introduce variety in the form of project work, other topics, other subjects, local problems, role-playing, visual material and so on.

Problem of the terminology

This problem is part of the previous problem. It would seem very natural for a teacher to complain that the CoRT terminology is unnecessary, since it calls by artificial names processes which are done anyway and can be called by more usual names. The artificial names tend to be regarded as jargon and are often not used by the teachers.

'If you give them the PMI they might think that it's different from actually doing the thinking in that direction, in that way, and they won't realize it's all just thinking.'

'Even the FIP or C & S are just one more damned thing to remember from their point of view. I didn't really get anywhere until I threw the teacher's handbook out of the window and began to look at our problems first, leaving out the jargon, but making up my own examples, getting them to do this and coming to the concept at the end.'

'Most teachers would be against jargon.'

'Only fifty per cent of them remembered what a CAF was; thirty per cent for C & S and seven per cent for AGO.'

'I feel it is a criticism of myself rather than the system – I am diffident about using the terminology – I am concerned about overplaying the hand.'

'There is no doubt that this use of abbreviations for getting the children to remember the lessons works.'

'I think I've detected that a new language has developed. For example in the discussion societies that we have here, a lot of these terms come up – to my surprise. Well, not a lot, but some. One girl, reading her paper to the rest of the school, said: "Considering the OPV of this . . ." and those not in the picture were baffled! For her it was already part of her vocabulary. Boys come to me and say: "Yes, sir, but from the CAF point of view, short-term, long-term and OPV," and all the rest of it. That is now part of their vocabulary. For them it's a word, so when I'm talking to them on any subject, I use the terminology. At first there were a few smiles, but now they're using it themselves.'

There is no doubt that teachers are shy about using the terminology: probably fearing the development of a private language that will be incomprehensible to anyone else. The first CoRT section has several of these artificial 'tools', but the second section has only one. Surprisingly those teachers who had complained about these tools in the first section later came back and said that they wished the same type of tool had been available in the second section! Since so many of these artificial tools are concentrated in the first section (so that they can be used in later sections) it must seem to the teacher that every lesson is going to contain a fresh bit of jargon. The problem is that unless the codes are used freely and in a matter-of-fact way they will always seem strange.

It does take time to get used to the terminology (the codes). In time teachers do find themselves using the expressions 'PMI' and 'CAF' without self-consciousness.

As explained at many different points in this book, the purpose of having these codes is to enable attention to be *held* in certain areas. It is not enough that a pupil should be thinking in a certain way. He should know that he is thinking in that way and be able deliberately to direct his thinking in that way. It is very much easier to say to a pupil, 'Do a PMI,' than to suppose that being a broad-minded person he will naturally look at the good and bad points – and to criticize him if he does not. It is also easier for the pupil to direct himself to 'do a PMI'.

It may seem easier and more natural to run the CoRT lessons without the special terminology. This is a short-sighted strategy, for the lessons will all seem the same and there will be no residue of transferable skill. Each lesson will seem to be a discussion session in which the pupils' natural thinking is used.

Problem of transfer

This is an important problem. It is not much use if the thinking skills are confined to the CoRT lessons: if the pupils regard the course as a closed situation in which certain games are expected.

'I think a problem is that the teachers in other subjects do not know about it.'

'Another student wanted to use the processes in other subjects but was concerned that if she did this other people wouldn't understand her.'

The transfer of thinking skills will be discussed in the results section. It seems that there is good transfer to such situations as English essays, but little overt transfer to other subjects. There does, however, seem to be more transfer to thinking situations outside school. So it seems possible that it is more a matter of the CoRT processes being shut out of other subjects than of their being locked into CoRT lessons.

It would be unreasonable to expect pupils to use the CoRT codes openly in other subjects. Hopefully they would use the codes *internally* as attention-focusing devices.

Problem of the practice items

The practice items provide another big problem area. But here the matter seems to be more a problem of expectation. Each lesson contains about eight practice items. There are sixty lessons, so there are 480 practice items. It is unlikely that each of those is going to be quite different. It is unlikely that every one of those items is going to be of immediate relevance or interest to each pupil. Since the CoRT material is designed as framework material that may be used with different ages, abilities and backgrounds, some of the more closely focused problems have to be omitted. For instance boy–girl problems may be of absorbing interest to sixteen-year-olds but are less interesting to ten-year-olds. By contrast, ten-year-olds could talk freely about marriage and the problems of marriage breakdown, whereas the sixteen-year-olds felt that such problems were too adult for them!

'Sometimes they'll discuss something that's really silly, like the badges to show your mood. It is not revelant to anything but they liked it.'

'They tend to go for things which are within their own experience.'

Pupil: 'The practice items should be related to situations in society around you.'

'Some children enjoy rather bizarre items like the spaceman approaching earth – but you should show the relevance.'

'Some items that were tackled with ease by eight-year-olds seemed to be too difficult for fourteen-year-olds.'

'Practice items tend to be a bit abstract. They don't seem to relate to you. They seem separate – for instance the yellow car one.'

'The practice items relate more to the young adolescent than they do to the primary child. If I go to sell this to my staff I meet with an initial resistance, because people are going to say this material is not designed for primary children -- to which I counter that the basic notion is applicable whether you are three or three hundred and thirty-three! They will accept that, but they all want some material which they can use and which relates to primary pupils as they know them, and this does not.'

'With many pupils the practice items are the only thing they have to hold on to, and wrong ones will turn them off.'

'The pupils particularly enjoyed using these processes on things of direct, personal interest to themselves; for instance the CAF on choosing a career was so successful that it ran into two weeks.'

'The main point is that many teachers have decided that they prefer their own ideas and themes, for many of the ideas in the leaflets are not making any impact on the kids. They don't understand the question or the idea really and they don't have any enthusiasm for it. There is perhaps one out of the five that you can start off with.'

It should be said at once that teachers are encouraged to invent their own practice items, especially if they are local or topical or of special interest to their own classes. In most lessons a range of practice items is given so that the teacher can choose the more suitable ones. Further alternatives are given in the handbook in the 'test' section.

The response of teachers to the practice items is so totally contradictory that it seems that it must often be based on expectation rather than fact. Exactly the same practice item that has been condemned by one teacher as being irrelevant is praised by another as having provided a good discussion. Pupils claim that they want items that are 'relevant' to their own lives, and yet they show more lively thinking on items that are not relevant. Pupils often tend to prefer items about which they are going to do no thinking. Instead they will bring out their prejudices and stereotyped ideas. If a problem is too close at hand it is not suitable for practising thinking. Teachers often complain that some items are too adult for younger children and yet, consistently, younger children show that they enjoy tackling problems of this sort.

In general it must be said that teachers' prejudices and preconceptions about the suitability of the items do not always accord with the facts shown by tape-recorded discussions. On the other hand the same practice item will be discussed with great interest by one group but will bore the group at a nearby table. It very often seems to depend on how the discussion gets started. It certainly depends on how the teacher 'sets up' the practice item.

The immediate world of children is fairly restricted and it would be very boring to discuss the same problems over and again. Furthermore there would be little objective and detached thinking practice. Ideally there should be a mix of items: some of them can be remote and abstract, others should be immediate and relevant.

It is important for the teacher to stress that a skilled thinker should be able to *think* about anything rather than just trotting out views he already holds on some matter.

It is a valid criticism that many of the practice items are about things that will happen in the 'future'. But thinking itself is usually speculative, in terms of taking action, making decisions and so on. Explanation and description are part of academic thinking, but in real life thinking is the prelude to action – and that affects the future.

In practical terms the teacher can try to do the following:

introduce as much variety and as many local items as possible

keep a mixture of items: some of immediate relevance, others more remote

remember that the purpose of the lessons is to practise thinking, not to reach conclusions about life's problems

introduce each item, whatever it is, in as interesting a manner as possible – by emphasizing the more interesting aspects

refrain from preconceptions about items that are 'suitable' or 'relevant' for particular age groups

rely more on the pupils' actual thinking behaviour than on what they *say* about the items.

Problem of 'drop-out'

In the discussion on the group format it was mentioned that in some cases members of the group would 'opt out' or 'drop out' and take no part in the discussion. This can happen not only with groups but in general. Some pupils do not seem to be interested in thinking about various things. But this problem probably arises less often than with other subjects, and it is surprising how many pupils are interested in thinking about things and offering their opinion. On the other hand the problem may be more noticeable in the thinking lessons, because pupils are *expected* to join in the discussion or offer ideas, whereas in a geography or history class they may quietly 'turn off' without anyone noticing.

'The atmosphere is that of children who enjoy the work. The worst that happens is that occasionally some child will opt out, then obviously there is nothing in it for him.'

'Not all kids are carried along in the discussion. Some just sit and dream.'

As suggested above, this problem is not peculiar to the subject of 'thinking', but occurs in any subject. In fact it may be somewhat easier to deal with in thinking lessons because the teacher can draw a pupil into a discussion by asking a question he is able to answer. Furthermore no special knowledge is required, so the pupil's response can be praised and elaborated in order to draw him into the lesson. The teacher can also try to find some aspect of the situation that does appeal to the uninterested pupils. Often this can be done by personalizing the situation: 'If you were in that position what would you do?' or: 'Has that ever happened to you? Tell us what you did.'

Problem of status

'The strongest motivation for sixteen-year-olds would be an exam, a mark or a comment on a report.'

There is no doubt that in many cases older pupils are very examination-conscious and chary of spending time or effort on anything which is not going to contribute directly to their examination performance. The way the subject is presented by the teacher, the place it occupies in the timetable and whether other classes have done the subject all affect its status. It has been noticed that when the subject has been taught to another class in the school before, it is much easier to get it accepted.

'I was a bit surprised when the second group came in because I thought the first group might have been rather anti, and that they might have passed the word round, and so the second group might have come in anti, but in fact they didn't. They settled down right away and started using the initials, and they seemed to enjoy it.'

The status of the subject is important. Giving status to a new subject is always a problem. It doesn't help to tuck the subject away in a corner or to make it replace some popular subject (such as art) or a free period.

Summary

Many of the major problems have been considered here. Some are common to any new curriculum subjects. Others arise from the open-ended nature of the subject. Yet others arise particularly from the CoRT approach. Some of the problems are created because teachers do not appreciate the purpose of the CoRT approach. They can overcome the problems first of all by recognizing them and then by making the necessary adjustments or adaptations. It must be remembered that the problems listed here were largely reported by teachers on their first exposure to the subject. In many cases (for example with the problem of introducing variety and emphasizing the distinctiveness of each lesson) further experience proved sufficient to solve the problem.

Tests and testing

No one has ever tested the ultimate value of teaching poetry or English literature or geography or history. It is taken for granted that they are part of education. We can test how well these subjects are taught or how well the pupil learns them, but not whether they are worth teaching. That is a matter of belief. We believe that being more aware of the world around us, of art and of history, must be a good thing. For the same reason we are beginning to teach social studies.

With 'thinking', however, it is different. Everyone thinks, therefore a course of thinking must be expected to show that it has improved thinking. Otherwise what is the point of devoting time to it? This is self-evident. But the trouble arises when we find that testing thinking is extraordinarily difficult and beset with pitfalls.

Standard tests

Because standard tests are objective we trust them. Because standard tests give us a numerical result we feel comfortable with them. Unfortunately what we rarely do is to question the applicability of the test. We tend to suppose that if the test is a good test then its application must be valid. There is a huge danger, however, in using inappropriate tests, and in the field of thinking one is very much aware of this danger. I have had several research schemata sent to me suggesting the use of totally inappropriate tests to test thinking skill. IQ tests manifestly require the exercise of thinking. But IQ tests are not a test of thinking. There should be no change in IQ after a course in training thinking skill. If such a change were to be measured this would automatically cast doubts on the validity of the IQ test as a measure of 'innate' intelligence.

Similarly the standard tests of verbal reasoning do not test the 'attention skills' developed in courses such as CoRT. All thinking involves an element of creativity, but a creativity test such as the Torrance test would be very unlikely to show a change after a course in thinking lessons – unless those lessons had been specifically designed to develop the particular skills that are tested by the test. It would be nonsense to compare the effects of a general course with a test-based course by using the test itself.

It must seem a convenient policy to reject the use of standardized tests that might show the ineffectualness of thinking courses. Unfortunately a test that is inappropriate does not suddenly become appropriate 'because it is the best thing we have', or 'because it is convenient to say it is inappropriate'. You do not measure a person's honesty by measuring his height, on the grounds that this is an objective, reliable measurement. In general we must be much more aware of the danger posed by the inappropriate use of standardized tests. The temptation is great. The tests are easy to use and the results will be credible. We badly need a test to test the applicability of standardized tests. Without such a pre-test it is a matter of surmise or philosophical speculation or trivial semantics.

Teaching the test

If you were teaching a girl to play the violin you would hardly test her skill by asking her to play the piano. Yet if you asked her to play the violin you would be accused of 'teaching the test'. There is a great deal of misunderstanding on this point. You can train people to do IQ tests by giving them a lot of practice, providing certain routines and focusing on the specific skills tested in an IQ test. The IQ test now becomes invalid as a test of that person's IQ for you have taught the test. For that person the IQ test will test only how well you have taught him to do IQ tests (plus the intelligence needed for the training). It is from situations like this that the horror of 'teaching the test' has arisen. If you do a careful survey of the examination papers in a medical school you may find that only a limited range of questions is ever asked. You teach your medical students those questions and they do well in the examinations. Again the examinations are no true test because you have taught the test.

On the other side of the matter you do not test violin-playing on the piano or medical knowledge by setting questions in mathematics or geographical knowledge by using a history examination paper. Where you are testing what you have taught it is perfectly appropriate to use a test that is very like the matters you have taught. It is not appropriate if the test is supposed to measure some innate quality like IQ or creativity.

How does this apply to the field of thinking? We tend to feel that thinking skill is an innate quality and that therefore the test should be remote and abstract and not resemble the material that has been taught. The thinking skill exhibited in a CoRT lesson on CoRT material may well have improved, but does this indicate an improved thinking skill in life outside the CoRT classes? The problem is one of transfer. If we teach thinking with abstract games and puzzles and simulations, it is no use testing the general improvement in thinking skill with games and puzzles, because that tells us nothing about transferable skills. But if we teach thinking with problems and situations that are very similar to those which the pupil is going to have to think about in the outside world (careers, social behaviour, relationship with parents, shopping), the difficulty does not arise. We can use these same areas to test any improvement in thinking skill. Ideally we should not continue to use the thinking situations in the abstract, classroom, pencil-and-paper mode, but in a real-life setting with the pupils standing in an employment exchange deciding whether to take a job or not. We should also like to see five or ten years later whether the pupil still shows any improved thinking skill on the way. Any test in a classroom is very far from this.

So, in testing a pupil's ability to think about certain types of problem, it is perfectly appropriate to use that type of problem.

Quantification

We invented numbers in order to make valid comparisons. We trust those comparisons that are expressed in numbers. In fact we trust quantification so much that we expose ourselves to three dangers. The first danger is that we attend only to those things that can be quantified and ignore the rest. It may be that the matters that can be quantified are not so important as the un-quantifiable ones. For example we can count the full-stops in an essay. That gives a reliable, objective, quantifiable measure. But it tells less about the value of the essay than other non-quantifiable aspects. The second danger is that we sometimes forget that at some stage a subjective impression may have been converted into an objective number. This happens very often in sociology: someone devises a five-point scale; a person is located on this scale by subjective judgement; but once on the scale the person becomes a figure, and the figures go to make up numbers, which are treated with all the respect usually accorded numbers. The third danger is that we accept it when statistics show us that something is 'significantly' greater than something else. We quickly forget the actual degree of difference. For example if I were to show that the IQ of porridge-reared children was three points higher than that of cornflakes-reared children (with statistical significance), it would quickly be forgotten that the difference was only three points, and only an average at that. It would be assumed very soon, that every porridge-reared child was much cleverer than every cornflakes child. Legislation and dietary control would be demanded.

Applying numbers to thinking is no easier than applying numbers to English essays. We can, of course, set up a number of artificial questions and see how many are answered at all or answered correctly. That is one way of generating numbers. We can do a large survey and see how most people think about a particular subject. We can then see how the thoughts of an individual compare to this 'average' thinking. But what do we measure? We can look at someone's thinking as expressed in an essay or on tape and pick out and count certain things. But what do we count?

It is impossible to count patterns unless we standardize those patterns so that they are recognizable in an objective way. The simplest pattern in thinking is probably an idea or, more simply, an area of attention. This has been the basic approach in testing the effect of the CoRT Thinking lessons.

The simple measurement of the number of ideas or attention-areas is appropriate because one of the intentions of the CoRT course (and especially of the first section, CoRT I) is to broaden the thinking of pupils. So a measurement of the 'scan' of that thinking in terms of the number of different attention-areas is in order. Most of the experiments to be discussed in the results section are based on this sort of measurement. It can be shown that CoRT-trained groups do cover a larger number of attention-areas than untrained groups.

As might be expected even this simple counting of ideas leads to problems. The counting is subjective. When is an idea an idea? When is an idea one or two ideas? How valuable are the ideas? How general and how specific are the ideas?

In doing a CAF (consider all factors) on a picnic, one boy lists the following:

picnic basket
knives and forks
plates
beer
soft drinks
sausages
hard-boiled eggs
salt and pepper
table-cloth or rug
bag for litter

Another boy tackles it differently:

The people who are coming on the picnic
the location

the transport
the weather
the food and equipment needed

The first boy seems to have twice as many 'ideas' as the second boy – or does he? Should the teacher lump all the first boy's ideas under the headings of food and equipment and tally only one idea? These are the sort of problems that arise. In addition to this problem of general and particular ideas there is the problem of intrinsic value. Should a pupil who, when asked to think about slum clearance, has considered the matters of traffic disruption, noise and dust, effect on local shopkeepers and style of new buildings, be given a higher mark than the pupil who has considered none of these things but has mentioned the disruption of social relations which the first pupil had omitted?

Further work is being carried out at the Cognitive Research Trust to try to overcome some of these problems and to devise different methods of testing improvements in thinking skill.

Subjective improvement

Unless there is an objective measure such as measuring the time taken to run a hundred metres, most exercises of skill tend to be assessed in a subjective manner (music, painting, architecture, cooking, English essays and so on). This is because the human mind is very sensitive even to complex patterns and can often recognize patterns it cannot describe objectively. Often these patterns are too complex to be broken down into separate measurable features.

There is no doubt that a teacher would be in the best position to assess any improvement in thinking skill. This improvement may involve such things as: being more willing to listen to others; being less dogmatic; being more prepared to think about things instead of dismissing them; asking better questions; being more 'mature' and so on. None of these things would be picked out by a standardized test or by idea-counting. The reason why we are reluctant to accept such subjective measurements is that we know how biased and unreliable such measurements can be.

We suspect that a teacher in favour of the material may 'notice' improvement more than another. Conversely a teacher who disagrees with the approach may notice less than he should. If the change is very gradual a teacher, or a pupil, might not notice anything even when there was an improvement. A teacher might be reluctant to admit that his teaching had been in vain and so might exaggerate the benefits. Outside assessment by an independent person could overcome many of these objections – provided the outside assessor knew what to look for.

A further possibility is randomized performance. For instance essays from a CoRT-trained group are randomly mixed with essays from an untrained group and the assessors are asked to mark the essays for their thinking content or to pick out the CoRT essays. The trouble here is that there may be clues (such as the use of a deliberate PMI format in the CoRT essays) which would render the random mixing useless.

Pattern recognition

Unconscious bias is more of a problem than conscious bias. If the observer has well-defined patterns that he can recognize with ease, then bias can be much diminished. After all, that is how art experts and antique dealers survive. They do make mistakes, but on the whole the pattern recognition they have built up with experience is reliable. If the assessor of thinking skill had some definite patterns which he could recognize with ease he would be reliable, and it would take a considerable amount of conscious bias to upset the assessment. So perhaps the most important step is to define and clarify certain basic patterns in thinking. We can then train people to pick out these patterns and use these trained people to detect changes in thinking skill. Again at the Cognitive Research Trust this is one of the directions in which the research is moving.

Comparison

Detecting improvements in thinking skill involves comparisons. You may compare a person's thinking after exposure to a course with his thinking before exposure. Several experiments of a 'cross-over' type have been conducted. A random half of a class would think about one problem and the other half about a second problem. At the end of ten lessons the two halves would tackle the problem they had not tackled the first time round. The thinking would then be compared in two ways: the before and after thinking of the same group but on different problems; the thinking of before and after random halves on the same problem. The difficulty with this type of testing in a school is that much can happen within a single term. Children mature or are exposed to different influences, for example on television. The result is that measurable effects are difficult to ascribe to the influence of the thinking course itself.

Parallel group comparison is preferable. Two groups are matched in age and ability (according to some standardized test). The performance of the CoRT-trained group is then compared directly with that of the untrained group (essay, notes, taped discussion). This is easier to do in thinking than in any other subject. You could not compare a group trained in French with a group who had had no training. But since thinking is something that everyone does in the normal course of his life, you can compare a CoRT-trained group with an untrained group to see if there is any difference in their thinking. Some problems arise when the CoRT group start using the CoRT processes in a deliberate manner, for this complicates the comparison.

Summary

Thinking is so complex a performance that it is difficult to test. It is most important that the test should be appropriate to the skills that have been taught. The intrinsic objectivity or reliability of a test is no measure at all of its applicability. Picking out and counting ideas or attention-areas may be appropriate in some cases, but there are difficulties. The teacher's assessment would be the most suitable, because it can embrace matters too subtle to show up in cut-and-dried tests. There is, however, the danger of conscious and unconscious bias (either way) and variability. Perhaps the ideal method would be to clarify a repertoire of definite thinking patterns and to use these as a basis of assessment – in the hands of a trained and experienced pattern-spotter.

Results

The results of teaching thinking directly as a skill will be examined in this section. The results discussed will be those that have followed the use of the CoRT programme. Some of the more general effects might equally well have followed any other programme for the teaching of thinking as a skill. Nevertheless it must be remembered that the CoRT programme is a real programme that has been used in a large number of schools and the results are actual results – it is not a matter of speculating what might happen. The results have followed from one or other aspect of the CoRT programme. The programme is a composite approach to the teaching of thinking and includes: perceptual approach; importance of attention and attention-directors; group work; variety of problems; achievement method; teaching style; specific 'attention' codes and so on. It would be wrong to assume that it was only the codes that mattered, or that the results arose directly from the codes.

There are two sorts of results that can be considered: soft data and hard data. The soft data include such things as: teachers' reports and comments; pupils' comments; anecdotes illustrating changes in thinking; actual changes in thinking behaviour in tape-recorded discussions; observed changes in English essays. Soft data tend to be complex and difficult to divide into quantifiable points. Provided that one can discount major bias I believe that soft data are more important than hard data. This is especially so with a complex subject like thinking. In fact the hard data (quantification, measurement, numbers) are surprisingly impressive, so the emphasis on soft data is not an excuse. Experiments are, however, very artificial. They measure only one part of the situation and only the circumstances of one group of tested pupils. In this section the soft data will be considered first, followed by some sample experiments showing the hard data.

Thinking behaviour

We tend to regard thinking as an intellectual exercise, but in practice it is a type of behaviour: both personal and social. When discussing a matter children tend to shout each other down; they call each other 'stupid' and 'daft', and what is said 'rubbish'; they refuse to listen on certain matters and refuse to think on others. This behaviour is not very much different from that of adults, except that the words used are not the same. Such behaviour is very often a substitute for thinking (shouting, voting) or a cover-up for an inability to think on a certain matter. When faced with a thinking situation many children have no confidence because they have had no practice. They do not know where to start. They do not have a framework to follow in order to produce ideas. Of course, it never occurs to those pupils that their thinking is in any way deficient because, being inside it, they cannot realize what is happening. Thinking is regarded as 'boring'. because they do not know how to go about it. They have no confidence in their own ideas because they have had no experience on which to base that confidence. Very few adults have ever been interested in listening to their ideas or asking them to think about things. All this is the general sort of background of behaviour of the pupils taking the CoRT Thinking lessons. The older and more able pupils differ in that they have often acquired a facility in knowledge regurgitation; a conceit in their cleverness; and a sort of 'debating' type of point-winning thinking. Their readiness to think about matters outside these areas – or indeed their skill – is not much different from the others'.

'From a teacher's point of view it was fascinating to watch their swing of opinion after full discussion; for instance the snap reaction to: "Every pupil should spend three months every year earning money," was to agree, but after the PMI practically everyone rejected the idea. Similarly they ended up by rejecting a special television channel for young people only.'

'The course seems to make them think more clearly. Makes them aware more generally – both in school work and in society in general.'

'Normally for a class discussion there are five who think and they say everything, and you sit there shutting them up, and encouraging someone else to say something. But in this there were only about four out of thirty-five who didn't say anything unless asked.'

'I would say it has widened their view of learning situations. They now realize that you can learn without having to write. I wouldn't say it has given them precise structures in thinking, but I'm pretty sure it has given them the ability to think abstractly about things a little more than they could before. I think it has pushed them on in that development to see other people's point of view.'

'The CoRT-trained group were much more able to work alone, whereas the untrained group were always wanting to work together, to say, "What did you get?" and so on. This was possibly due to practice. At the same time they could also get together and discuss things better. This trained group came up with varied approaches to the problem. [The suggestion had been that the police might go on strike.] They looked at what the government would say, sort of OPV. They looked at all the factors and the consequences. The boys in the untrained group were stuck in the rut of saying there'd be more crime, more murders, more "breaking", more robberies and variations on that. The boys in the trained group seemed to be suggesting that the government couldn't stand for it, they just couldn't leave the country to that situation. They would have to bring in the army and they would have to follow suit. They went on to ask what would happen to all their uniforms if they were out for a long time. They considered all the different aspects of it, whereas the other boys, even when listening to the trained group, seemed to be stuck. The trained group would go off to another point of view.'

'From the course the pupils have learned to think faster, to articulate ideas, to think more clearly. I think this might be an interplay of the CoRT lessons and the English taken together.

'As the weeks went by thinking did improve. There were more ideas. And more people were thinking.'

'The children have gained in confidence. The number of ideas has increased and we now get more refreshing ideas – not just the obvious ones.'

'It was remarked that the classes which had done the CoRT lessons seemed much more sensible in sex-education classes.'

'I would say from my own experience that it has definitely had an effect on the children. Quite a large number of them do actually see the implications of it.'

'I think it has affected teachers as well as children.'

'I have found that the great boon is that *everybody* gets something out of it.'

It has been noted by a teacher that the children who have done the CoRT lessons seem to behave more like a 'child from a good home background'. If this were true it would be of great importance, for few things in education ever make up for a poor home background. Yet in matters of confidence, listening to ideas and discussion it is possible to see how the thinking lessons might begin to have this effect.

In many cases the general change in thinking behaviour can be observed if we listen to tape-recorded discussions. The pupils who have had some CoRT practice tend to show the following differences:

No long gaps or pauses or 'What shall we say next?'

No wandering off by making one remark the starting-point for a totally irrelevant new remark and so on in classical 'point-to-point' fashion

Less giggling and whispering

More listening to other people and less talking across other people

Less direct abuse, shouting down, voting down or swamping of a different point of view; an occasional appreciation – 'That's a good point'

Readiness to think about any subject put before them instead of attacking it as boring or ridiculous and 'turning off'

Fewer initial judgements with thinking used only to back up these judgements, instead of to explore the matter

Less egocentricity

Seeming to know what to do next instead of just waiting for inspiration

The feeling that there is always more that can be said on the subject, in contrast to the feeling that everything possible has already been said.

No doubt many of these general effects arise simply from the fact that the pupils have been brought together from time to time to discuss and think about matters outside the usual curriculum. Much of the improvement is improvement in the social behaviour of discussion and group work. This is, of course, part of thinking and part of the thinking lessons. The ability to express ideas, confidence and fluency also arise from the practice in expressing ideas and hearing them expressed. In many respects the value of the CoRT lessons lies not so much in what is 'put in' to the lessons as in what is 'shut out' from the lessons. The deliberate attempt to exclude knowledge content with its own hierarchy and momentum is important. The deliberate attempt to focus on the process of thinking rather than on the content of the problem is also important. In discussion classes that are run as 'interest' classes with lengthy discussions on particular topics the effects tend to be different. In such groups the people taking part tend to get dogmatic, opinionated and controversial in their thinking. They tend to defend positions and make debating points. This is quite different from the more open thinking behaviour of the CoRT groups which are not trained on 'interest' discussions. This is a very important point, for too often we consider that such discussion sessions are good training in thinking.

Changes in ability

Several teachers have reported that pupils who had hitherto been regarded as backward in the academic subjects suddenly seemed to take an interest and shine in the CoRT Thinking lessons. It may have been that some particular practice item attracted the pupil's attention more than an academic matter had ever done. It may be that in the thinking lessons he found that the teacher actually listened to his idea and even praised it. It may be that in the thinking lesson he found for the first time that he actually had something to say.

In academic subjects there is a relentless flow of knowledge and if you fall behind at one point you are for ever struggling just to catch up. You are not able to contribute anything because you are not even abreast of the knowledge. With the CoRT lessons it is very different. Each lesson is separate and a pupil can start afresh with each lesson. He can come in and contribute something on one item in that lesson without ever feeling that he has been left behind.

In academic subjects the pupil has to take in a great deal of knowledge before he can start functioning by sifting and sorting that knowledge and handing it back to the teacher. Any pupil who is weak on this input side, through lack of attention or interest or little ability to store information, is at a disadvantage and cannot *begin* to function. In the CoRT lessons there is no 'input' side that has to be assimilated beyond the simple process. All pupils can start functioning equally. They already use the experience in their heads and their thinking to put things together. Thus for the first time a pupil's thinking gets a chance to shine on its own, without having to exhibit absorbed knowledge.

'I have found up to now that everyone is getting something out of it. And, from time to time, in written work, you get rather an unusual shaft of penetration from someone you didn't think was capable of it.'

'Johnny has always been behind the others in his school work.

In the CoRT lessons he blossomed as a thinker and surprised me as his teacher. What is more interesting is that he surprised the other children, who developed a new respect for him.'

'The more able children tend to give a greater number of responses, and perhaps the more interesting, less obvious ones. This is not always so: one of the little bonuses that comes out of this work is that some children that you know have a struggle with school work, will surprise you with the quality of the ideas they give to their group. But they tend to be the exception rather than the rule. It is arguable that for those particular children there is a social advantage in their being able to achieve at a higher level than they do in other subject areas.'

'I have noticed the most startling effects with the remedial children. It was very difficult at first to get going, but now there is a big change. They are prepared to stand up and *give* their ideas. They will now write at some length.'

Transfer

How much transfer is there? This is a question of great importance. This is the question everyone always asks. It is possible to show vastly improved performance in the CoRT lessons and on CoRT matters, but unless the thinking skill can be transferred to other situations it is not a very useful skill.

Many of the general effects mentioned earlier in this section do seem to transfer to other situations, but it is difficult to be sure because they are so general. A comprehensive school notes that the current year's intake from a primary school seems much brighter and more mature – it so happens that for the first time they had done the CoRT lessons.

The detection of transfer is very difficult, especially when the change in thinking skill is subtle and gradual. Obviously if the pupils rushed round saying 'PMI' on every occasion then the transfer would be obvious; but the transfer effects are more subtle.

In some cases the actual codes have been taught in such a thorough manner that they become part of the language:

'There was a very complicated cause of friction over a cricket bat, which I settled by using our terms – and they accepted the terms. If I appeal to a boy using the OPV it gets home to him. In brief, the terms seem to clarify a whole area of thought in a boy's mind. A whole nebulous area was clarified just by the use of one term. And the two boys in question were in 2B and not very clever. Previously this sort of thing used to take a long time to deal with. There was very little emotion, despite the fact that the boy whose bat was cracked was very upset. The conversation was so objective, so detached and so reasonable.'

In most cases, however, teachers have been diffident about over-playing the codes and as a result few of the codes (other than PMI, CAF, and perhaps OPV) are remembered or used consciously. Nevertheless the codes serve their purpose by holding attention on a process long enough to get it practised and to provide a structure for thinking during the lessons.

'I have just marked an essay on "Being a member of a Team" by a fifteen-year-old boy. He graphically described his physical fear of representing his school in his first away rugby match. He ended up by referring to the selection meeting he had originally attended which decided his fate as a full back – regretting that he had gone to the meeting. His last sentences were: "If I had known how to think about consequences and objectives I wouldn't have gone to the meeting. But I hadn't done the CoRT Thinking lessons then ..."'

'Each one has used these strategies in exams, essay questions, dealing with problems and so on.'

'I find that the pupils have used the processes even when not asked to do so.'

'I thought there would be no transfer of the processes outside the lessons and was not surprised, since it had not been set up for this. But as the weeks went by the thinking did improve and there were more ideas. The ideas tended to be the same in structure or in the way they came up with them, but there were more ideas.'

'I certainly had more children who said "yes". They used it elsewhere in other situations, for instance in English essays.'

'Two of the other younger children actually went home and

told their elder sisters about the thinking lessons, and the older sisters have been learning from the younger sisters, which I think is very interesting.'

'Another student asked if she could buy the lessons to take them home to her parents.'

'I don't find myself using the processes in other subjects, but I do in discussions I have with people.'

'On questioning them afterwards several interesting points emerged. They agreed unanimously that the course made them think more deeply *during the actual lesson*; they agreed equally unanimously that they were *not* conscious of using this thinking process in other school subjects. An interesting corollary to this is that forty-two out of sixty (just over two-thirds) said that they had consciously used the process *outside* school when making decisions about buying something. One family decided not to buy a freezer after their daughter had done a combined PMI and CAF on it with them!'

It seems that there is good direct or indirect transfer to English essays and teachers often pick up the effect here. But unless a deliberate effort is made the transfer to other subjects is poor. This seems to be because the 'thinking processes' are *shut out* because they are not perceived to be part of the internal game of that subject. It is also likely that, while CoRT is a new subject, pupils feel that they would not be understood if they were to use the CoRT processes elsewhere. The transfer to situations outside school seems good, however. This is important because it supports the view that CoRT thinking is *shut out* of other subjects rather than being *shut in* to the CoRT lessons. It seems that the other subjects, more than the CoRT lessons are seen to be closed performance areas. This problem may be overcome with the increasing use of integrated studies and interdisciplinary inquiry; with more teachers using CoRT; with teachers using CoRT in their own subject areas; with the younger pupils taking CoRT as a foundation subject; and in general with the establishment of the idea of teaching thinking as a subject.

Experiments

A sample of experiments is shown and discussed here. The problems of conducting experiments in thinking have been discussed in the preceding section. The experiments reported here are of the 'idea-counting type', since they apply mainly to the first CoRT section, which is specifically concerned with broadening the scan of thinking so that more points come under attention. The advantages and disadvantages of this method have also been discussed in the preceding section. The experiments do not succeed in proving anything, because in each case it is always possible that a special set of circumstances biased the results. For instance, if the CoRT group felt that they were being asked to give a CoRT-type response their performance on the problem is no indication of a general transference effect. Some other experiments are described in earlier sections of the book. Much work is still going on in this area and much work remains to be done.

Experiment 1

Primary-school children, aged ten to eleven. Eight groups, four CoRT trained (ten lessons) and four untrained. Tape-recorded discussion with extraction of points by researcher who did not know which groups were which.

Comment on Experiment 1

The difference between the untrained group and the CoRT group is particularly striking. The CoRT groups covered a much wider 'scan' of areas. For example each of the CoRT groups looked at teaching-career prospects, but none of the untrained group did so. Again each of the CoRT groups regarded going abroad as an opportunity to learn languages but none of the untrained groups did so.

It must be remarked that the teacher who had been teaching CoRT to this group was an exceptionally good teacher. It is also very likely that the base-line improvement with young children is likely to be more striking than with older children, because they are less used to sitting and discussing things, so training in this will show more clearly.

Problem: 'A schoolgirl wants to train to be a teacher. Her father has to live abroad for five years because of his work, and her mother is going with him. Should the girl go with them or stay with relatives or friends so that she can finish school and do the training?' (The school contains many army children, so the problem is relevant.)

Points considered	Untrained groups				CoRT groups			
	1	2	3	4	1	2	3	4
language				x	x	x	x	x
girl's likes and dislikes (food etc.)		x				x		
opportunities abroad or at home	x	x		x		x	x	x
parents' attitude		x			x	x	x	x
practical difficulties abroad					x	x	x	x
practical difficulties at home		x						
girl's age and maturity			x			x		
climate	x	x				x	x	
cost of living alone and training				x		x	x	x
would parents have a home abroad?					x	x		x
other members of family					x			
cost of going abroad					x	x	x	
keeping in touch with parents		x	x		x		x	x
teaching–career prospects					x	x	x	x
training prospects					x	x		
having congenial friends		x				x		
holidays with parents		x			x		x	x
return to train after short stay	x				x	x		
go abroad after training			x			x	x	
father go abroad alone					x			

	1	2	3	4	1	2	3	4
teach (and train) abroad							x	x
parents visit her in holidays								x
lose contact with friends			x			x		
employment difficulties					x	x		x
opportunity to learn new languages					x	x	x	x
opportunity to make new friends						x		
unsettling effect of changing jobs					x		x	
parents' anxiety					x		x	
risk of exam failure							x	
able to support parents on return					x			
able to keep on family home						x		
TOTALS	3	5	5	5	17	17	19	13

Experiment 2

Village college. Mixed-ability pupils, aged twelve to thirteen years. Three groups that had done twelve lessons were compared with three untrained groups from a comparable class. Four pupils in each group. Tape-recorded discussion with extraction of points.

Problem: 'In order to make better use of scarce educational resources (i.e. money for education) there are two suggestions: schools in country areas should be closed – or schools should have fewer teachers. What do you think?'

Points considered	Untrained groups			CoRT groups		
	1	2	3	1	2	3
transport costs would increase		x		x	x	x
extra transport would increase rush-hour congestion				x	x	
extra transport would increase school's insurance premiums					x	
sick children would find it more difficult to get home from school					x	
travel sickness among commuting pupils					x	

	1	2	3	1	2	3
more staff needed in city schools				x	x	
crowded city schools difficult to organize						x
bad discipline would result in city schools			x	x	x	x
city schools would need enlarging				x	x	
city-school classes would be too large to teach		x	x	x	x	
slow learners at city schools would get less attention			x	x		
closing country schools would waste existing buildings			x	x		x
evening classes at country schools would cease	x			x		x
large comprehensive schools may be more efficient					x	
close pupil–staff contact at small schools is good	x		x			x
other users of country schools would object						x
country schools have social value to community						x
parents at evening classes in contact with school						x
with fewer teachers standards would decline		x	x	x		
fewer teachers – overworked staff				x		x
fewer teachers – fewer subjects possible					x	
overcrowding in city schools increases accidents				x	x	
parental opposition to children travelling in cities					x	
more truancy at large city schools				x	x	
reduction of teaching staff would create unemployment					x	
understaffing already exists in some schools	x					x
fewer teachers – pupils would have too much influence						x
teachers would leave profession if conditions worsen						x

	1	2	3	1	2	3
insufficient time to mark work properly						x
poorer exam results with fewer teachers						x
greater boredom with fewer teachers doing the subjects						x
further decentralization may be more efficient	x			x		
better use could be made of existing classrooms				x		
lower the school-leaving age		x		x		
improve teaching efficiency				x		
extend school facilities (paid evening classes)			x	x		x
make only essential subjects compulsory	x			x		
abolish grammar schools (cut transport costs)					x	
close boarding schools					x	
decentralize allocation of funds	x					
reduce overlap between primary and secondary work	x					
use school facilities for private study	x					
combine catering and meals-on-wheels for the old						x
open public restaurant in school canteen						x
use facilities (e.g. buses) for pensioners						x
encourage pupils to assist in services to pensioners						x
encourage pupils to provide entertainment for aged		x				x
hold remedial classes after school hours						x
fewer playing fields			x			
fewer books for library			x			
school market-garden project to raise funds			x			
increase charges (fines) for school library			x			
make children pay for exercise books			x			
remove subsidies on school dinners			x			
TOTALS	8	4	14	20	17	23

Comment on Experiment 2

The difference in the number of ideas or attention areas between the untrained and the CoRT groups is again apparent. It is interesting to note that when a group hits on a 'theme', then several ideas follow on this theme. Although the CoRT groups have more ideas they do not all have the same ideas. The ideas deal with the consequences of the suggestions and also offer alternative ways of saving or raising more money. No definite conclusion was reached or asked for.

Experiment 3

Village college. Mixed-ability pupils, twelve to thirteen years. Chosen to represent a scatter of ability. Ten pupils had done 10 CoRT lessons; the others were untrained. Tape-recorded interview with each pupil by research worker.

Problem: the following ten questions

a   *If your parents are thinking of moving away and they ask your opinion, what do you think you would say?*

b   *Should children be allowed to do as they like at home?*

c   *Should television last for only two or three hours as in Norway, where it doesn't usually start before 8 pm?*

d   *Do you think that children should be allowed to choose which subjects they do at school?*

e   *Do you think it was right to raise the school-leaving age to sixteen?*

f   *If you were a headmaster, how would you choose a new teacher?*

g   *What do you think people would say if you reported a pupil for beating up another boy?*

h   *If your class wanted to have a trip to the seaside and the warden hadn't time to arrange it, what would you do?*

i   If you were offered two holiday jobs, one in a shop and quite well paid, the other delivering newspapers, but not so well paid, which would you choose?

j   A friend of yours has stolen something, but you are accused. What can you do?

The following table shows the number of relevant points in the pupils' answers to each question.

CoRT group	Questions										Totals
	a	b	c	d	e	f	g	h	i	j	
Sally	8	4	3	3	2	7	3	5	4	2	41
Debra	2	3	3	3	3	3	3	7	3	3	33
Sylvia	4	3	3	3	2	4	4	2	3	3	31
Jennifer	3	2	2	2	3	3	2	5	4	3	29
Helen	4	2	2	2	1	4	3	3	5	3	29
Eric	3	1	2	2	4	5	2	2	3	2	26
Alan	4	2	3	1	2	4	3	3	2	1	25
Michael	1	2	3	2	2	4	4	2	2	1	23
Tina	3	1	3	2	2	2	2	1	2	2	20
Nicholas	1	1	1	2	1	3	1	1	2	1	14
											271

Untrained group	Questions										Totals
	a	b	c	d	e	f	g	h	i	j	
Denise	2	2	2	3	1	3	1	6	2	2	24
Keith	1	1	2	2	2	3	3	5	2	2	23
Geoffrey	4	1	3	1	2	3	2	1	1	2	20
Rosemary	2	2	2	2	2	2	2	1	2	2	19
Steven	2	2	1	2	1	3	2	2	2	1	18
Karen	4	1	1	1	2	2	2	1	2	2	18
Karina	4	1	1	1	2	1	1	3	2	2	18
Judith	3	2	1	2	1	2	2	1	1	2	17
Brenda	1	1	1	1	1	2	3	3	1	2	16
Nicola	2	1	2	1	1	3	2	1	2	1	16
											189

Comment on Experiment 3

This experiment is of particular interest, since so many of the other experiments deal with 'group' results and it may be argued that any improved thinking performance is only a matter of improved group dynamics through practice. In this experiment the individual output of ideas has been measured and it can be seen that there has been an improvement in almost all cases. Not one of the untrained groups produced as many ideas as the average for the CoRT group. All except one of the CoRT group exceed the average for the untrained group. In the untrained group only two out of the ten have a total of more than twenty ideas spread across the various questions. In the CoRT group eight out of ten have more than twenty ideas.

Experiment 4

Comprehensive school, mixed-ability groups, fourteen years average age. The CoRT-trained groups had done fifteen lessons. Total number of students: forty-seven. Twenty-minute discussion in tape-recorded groups with extraction of ideas.

Problem: 'How would you reorganize the local bus service to improve it?'

Broad idea areas	Untrained groups				CoRT groups			
	1	2	3	4	1	2	3	4
Vehicles	3	4	7	1	4	9	15	3
Routes	6	3	1	0	6	2	3	2
Passengers	2	3	1	1	3	3	2	2
Timetables	6	2	1	1	7	3	2	1
Fares	2	1	1	1	3	1	3	2
Other points	3	2	1	1	2	3	4	3
GROUP TOTALS	22	15	12	5	25	21	29	13
		(total 54)				(total 88)		

Comment on Experiment 4

The teacher had arranged the groups in descending order of ability so that in each case group 1 was the most able and group 4 the least able. It is possible to see that in each case the CoRT-trained group did better than the untrained group, although the best performing group had not been judged the most able in the CoRT group. This highlights the difficulty of assessing thinking performance, for a sudden spate of ideas in one area can have a considerable effect on the idea count.

Experiment 5

Middle school, mixed ability, age fourteen years. The CoRT trained groups (group 1 had nineteen pupils, group 2 had twenty pupils) had done five CoRT lessons and were matched with equivalent pupils who had done no training. The output was in an unspecified written form. The teacher and the research worker extracted the points in parallel. The points from individual pupils were finally added together to give overall figures.

Problem: 'Is it a good idea for people with more children to pay less tax?'
(For one of the pairs of groups the question was posed as: 'Is it a bad idea . . .' but this made no apparent difference to the way it was answered and the figures below refer to the positive version, which is the way the pupils treated it.)

		Untrained groups		CoRT groups	
		1	2	1	2
initial judgements;	positive	13	17	8	10
	negative	2	0	2	2
	TOTALS	15	17	10	12

continued on page 252

	1	2	3	4
points in favour of idea	17	23	27	28
points against idea	5	8	23	20
total judgement points	22	31	50	48
neutral (non-judgement) points	22	0	10	17
Comparison of point count done by teacher with that done by research worker: average number of points per pupil:				
teacher	2·3	2·0	3·2	2·9
research worker	2·4	2·4	3·2	3·3

Comment on Experiment 5

As usual the CoRT-trained group produced more ideas both in favour of and against the idea. What is most striking is that the CoRT training seemed to make a considerable difference to a pupil's ability to generate ideas contrary to his own feeling on the matter. Thus the CoRT groups have many more points against the idea than the untrained groups, which mainly give points in favour. This supports the idea that CoRT training helps to create detachment. For the same reasons the CoRT groups made fewer initial judgements because they had been trained to explore rather than judge. The comparison of the teacher's and the research worker's point count is interesting.

Experiment 6

Girls' high school; aged thirteen to fourteen years. A CoRT-trained class of thirty-two pupils had done just *one* lesson and was compared with a comparable class (also thirty-two pupils) which had done no CoRT lessons. The output was in the form of an English essay. Point extraction by research worker.

Problem: 'Do you think there should be special weekend prisons for minor offenders?'

	Untrained group	CoRT group
points in favour of the idea	47	81
points against the idea	56	119
total number of points	105	200
average number of points per pupil	3·3	6·2
distinct points in favour of the idea	17	31
distinct points against the idea	19	36
	36	67
arguments put against declared verdict as percentage of arguments in favour of that verdict*	20·5	58·7

* In the CoRT class 23 pupils put 80 arguments in support of their verdict and 47 against. In the 'untrained' class 28 pupils put 70 arguments in favour of their verdict and 16 against.

Comment on Experiment 6

This experiment supports the previous one in showing that the CoRT-trained group were more able to generate points which were on the opposite side to their own conclusions about the situation. As before, more ideas were generated both against the idea and in favour of it. This applied both to the total volume of points and to the distinct or separate points. It is interesting to note that this effect was produced after one lesson (the PMI lesson). It is possible that the experiment was run too soon after the lesson and so the effect may not persist.

Experiment 7

Public school, boys aged fifteen years. Twenty boys in a cross-over experiment. Nine boys tackled problem A and eleven tackled problem B. Both groups were then given 20 CoRT lessons (CoRT I and II). The same groups then tackled the problem they had not tackled before. The output was written in note form. The 'before' and 'after' comparison was made for each problem and this is referred to as 'untrained' and 'CoRT' (i.e. post-CoRT). Three months elapsed between the two tests.

Problems:

A 'Discuss the idea of everyone doing some social work before taking a job.'

B 'What can be done about necessary but unpleasant jobs (such as mining and refuse collecting) that no one wants to do?'

Problem A

Areas	Untrained groups	CoRT groups
impact on individuals	30	32
impact on those helped	11	12
impact on social services	2	9
impact on society as a whole	1	9
impact on economy and politics	1	18
problems of organization	1	8
total number of distinct ideas (points)	16	29
average number of points per pupil	5·7	9·7
average number of areas used by a pupil	2·5	4·7
average number of original points*	1·4	3·2

* An idea that was unique or shared by only one other in the group.

Problem B

Areas	Untrained groups	CoRT groups
workers' viewpoint	13	17
nature of work	11	17
change of work	3	8
change labour	4	6
consequences for economy	5	8
attitudes	2	2
government attitudes	0	1
total number of distinct ideas (points)	12	18
average number of points per pupil	3·7	6·7
average number of areas used by a pupil	2·9	3·8
average number of original points	0·6	2·1

Comment on Experiment 7

The total figures given refer to distinct points, whereas the average per pupil refers to total points. It may be seen that in each case there is a considerable increase in the total number of points per pupil, in the original points and in the areas covered. The first problem about doing social work has been used on a number of other occasions and has given consistent results, showing that the CoRT-trained group do not produce many more ideas than the untrained group in the area of egocentric ideas, but that the difference grows very large as one moves away from egocentric ideas to considering the effect on society or the practical administration of the idea. For example the CoRT group produced eighteen ideas relating the effect of the suggestion to the economy and politics, whereas the untrained group could offer only one.

Experiment 8

Comprehensive school. The CoRT group had done ten CoRT lessons in addition to their normal interdisciplinary inquiry. The untrained group from a similar school in the area had done only the interdisciplinary inquiry without using CoRT as a core subject. The output was in essay form. Extraction of points by research worker.

Problem: 'Should a company making shoes change its styles as often as it can?'

	Untrained group	CoRT group
average mental age	11·67	11·59
average chronological age	11·83	11·90
number of pupils	20	20
boys	15	16
girls	5	4
total number of points made	168	227
percentage of points that were: particular*	20	4
anecdotal†	24	6
percentage of individuals making initial judgement	100	15
average number of areas covered‡	3·9	4·5
number using less than 4 areas	8	1

* A particular point is one that refers to a detailed example or instance.
† An anecdotal point refers to an incident or story (e.g.: 'If a girl bought high-heeled shoes and then fell over . . .').
‡ Six main areas of attention were extracted from the responses (e.g. effect on people, cost of production etc.).

Comment on Experiment 8

As in the preceding experiments the CoRT group shows a greater total of points. If, however, we start to look at the type of points used we find that the untrained group were more likely to make up their point totals with detail and anecdote. We also find that the untrained group were more likely to get their points in a few

areas and not to scan across the field. In the CoRT group all
except one covered five out of the six available areas.

This experiment shows the limitation of the method of counting points, which tends to underestimate the improvement in scan
of the CoRT-trained groups.

General comments on the experiments

Taken as a whole the experiments that involved point-counting
(including the many not mentioned here), show the following:

The CoRT training effect is more visible with younger and less
able children, because older children are usually able to produce
some ideas even if they are all in the same area.

CoRT training leads to a wider spread of ideas over the different
areas. It also leads to ideas that are more general in nature and
less particular or anecdotal.

The strongest effects are to be seen as one moves out of the egocentric and immediate-attention areas to consider wider effects
and practical matters. Ordinary thinking is reluctant to look at
things in so wide a manner, and hence the CoRT effect is strong.

When time is short and the pupils have a lot to say on some
subject, the effect of the CoRT training may not be apparent in
a simple idea count, because the pupils are limited by time, not
by lack of ideas.

CoRT-trained pupils make fewer initial and instant judgements.

CoRT-trained pupils are more inclined to generate points on
both sides of the question instead of restricting their thinking to
the side they favour. They offer a better exploratory balance
between 'for' and 'against' points.

Conclusion

This book has been about the deliberate teaching of thinking as a skill and its practical implementation as a curriculum subject. The first part of the book was about the nature of thinking. This first part sought to clarify the complex process of thinking and to shift the emphasis from logic to perception. The second part of the book described a practical, on-going attempt to teach thinking directly as a school subject. No doubt there is much wrong with the approach and the programme. Nevertheless it is a practical programme that is in use. No matter how imperfect it may be, something that is actually in use can tell us more about the teaching of thinking than any amount of theory or 'test-tube' experimentation.

In this section, as a sort of summary, I shall pick out the main points of the book.

Complacency

We are very smug and complacent about our thinking skills. We feel that if we string two or three ideas together in a more or less logical fashion, avoid crass logical errors and express the ideas fluently, then we are skilled thinkers. The very important point to remember is that error-free thinking is not necessarily good thinking.

Logic and perception

Hitherto, in the matter of thinking, we have put all the emphasis on logic. But in most ordinary situations perception has to bear the brunt of thinking. If we are not looking in the right direction or do not have the right concepts no amount of logic will help us. To improve our skill in thinking we need to develop deliberate perceptual skills. Both logic and perception are required. It is only the arrogance of logic that is limiting.

Deliberate effort

If we are to improve our thinking skills we must make a deliberate effort: first to pay direct attention to this area and second to do something about it. Thinking skills will not improve by them-selves, or in the course of a general improvement in education. We have only to consider the thinking skills of the 'best'-educated to see that education does not yet pay enough direct attention to thinking skills – but hopes they will develop along the way. For-tunately the reaction of heads and teachers suggests that people at the active end of education are well aware of this problem.

Content and process

It is not enough to have general-interest discussions and to hope that transferable thinking skills will be developed in this manner. The process of abstraction and generalization is difficult at the best of times and competes but weakly with content interest. Atten-tion must be paid directly to the processes. It may even be neces-sary to make these 'unobvious' enough to get the attention they deserve.

The 'hump' effect

There is no reason at all to suppose that, from the start, the teaching of thinking will be easy, or that it will be rapturously received by the pupils. It may be necessary to go 'uphill' for a while and face awkwardness and other difficulties before things settle down on the other side of the hump.

Teacher dependence

There can be no doubt that the successful teaching of thinking as a skill depends very largely on the teacher. At best any material can only provide a framework within which he can work. He has to be interested in the subject and has to give it the status which pupils require. He has to develop a teaching skill suited to an open-ended subject, and in particular to develop ways of giving pupils a sense of achievement. Finally he has to believe that it is worthwhile, and then has to be *determined* to make it work. The subject is too important to be handled in a tentative or dabbling manner. Although much is demanded of the teacher the opportunity for rewarding teaching is great.

Acknowledgements

Although this book is about the practical teaching of thinking as a skill and not about the CoRT Thinking programme, most of the practical observations are based on the operation of that programme. I should therefore like to express my thanks and appreciation to those organizations and people who have been involved in the project. I am especially appreciative of the initial grant given by the Leverhulme Foundation, which enabled the project to get started and continues to sustain it. More recently the Wates Foundation have also provided a grant. The organization and research work has been done, over the years, by a number of people whose contribution I should like to acknowledge here: David Tripp, Edna Copley, Christine McKenzie, Brian Oliver, Audrey Davies, Penny Skae and Clare Connell.

I must also thank all those teachers and heads whose actual work on the project exceeded our own, since the application of a framework is very much harder work than merely providing it.

Index

FOR THE BEST IN PAPERBACKS, LOOK FOR THE (🐧)

In every corner of the world, on every subject under the sun, Penguin represents quality and variety – the very best in publishing today.

For complete information about books available from Penguin – including Puffins, Penguin Classics and Arkana – and how to order them, write to us at the appropriate address below. Please note that for copyright reasons the selection of books varies from country to country.

In the United Kingdom: Please write to *Dept E.P., Penguin Books Ltd, Harmondsworth, Middlesex, UB7 0DA.*

If you have any difficulty in obtaining a title, please send your order with the correct money, plus ten per cent for postage and packaging, to *PO Box No 11, West Drayton, Middlesex*

In the United States: Please write to *Dept BA, Penguin, 299 Murray Hill Parkway, East Rutherford, New Jersey 07073*

In Canada: Please write to *Penguin Books Canada Ltd, 2801 John Street, Markham, Ontario L3R 1B4*

In Australia: Please write to the *Marketing Department, Penguin Books Australia Ltd, P.O. Box 257, Ringwood, Victoria 3134*

In New Zealand: Please write to the *Marketing Department, Penguin Books (NZ) Ltd, Private Bag, Takapuna, Auckland 9*

In India: Please write to *Penguin Overseas Ltd, 706 Eros Apartments, 56 Nehru Place, New Delhi, 110019*

In the Netherlands: Please write to *Penguin Books Netherlands B.V., Postbus 195, NL–1380AD Weesp*

In West Germany: Please write to *Penguin Books Ltd, Friedrichstrasse 10–12, D–6000 Frankfurt/Main 1*

In Spain: Please write to *Alhambra Longman S.A., Fernandez de la Hoz 9, E–28010 Madrid*

In Italy: Please write to *Penguin Italia s.r.l., Via Como 4, I-20096 Pioltello (Milano)*

In France: Please write to *Penguin Books Ltd, 39 Rue de Montmorency, F-75003 Paris*

In Japan: Please write to *Longman Penguin Japan Co Ltd, Yamaguchi Building, 2–12–9 Kanda Jimbocho, Chiyoda-Ku, Tokyo 101*

I Am Right – You Are Wrong

In this book Dr Edward de Bono puts forward a direct challenge to what he calls the rock logic of Western thinking. Rock logic is based on rigid categories, absolutes, argument and adversarial point scoring. Instead he proposes the water logic of perception. Drawing on our understanding of the brain as a self-organizing information system, Dr de Bono shows that perception is the key to more constructive thinking and the serious creativity of design.

The Happiness Purpose

Lucid, entertaining and provocative as always, Edward de Bono presents his blueprint for the disciplined pursuit of happiness which, in his opinion, is the legitimate purpose of life. Self-respect, dignity, self importance and humour occupy an important place in his scheme, and in this practical manual he shows how to utilize these assets as tools for mental and spiritual betterment.

Edward de Bono's Masterthinker's Handbook

It is never enough just to want to think or to exhort someone to think. What are the steps? What is to be done? Avoiding error and winning arguments is only a tiny part of thinking. The main enemies of thinking are confusion, inertia and not knowing what to do next. The 'Body' framework designed by Edward de Bono overcomes these problems.

Wordpower

Could you make an *educated guess* at the *downside-risk* of a *marketing strategy*? Are you in the right *ball-game*, and faced with a crisis could you find an *ad hoc* solution? These are just a few of the 265 specialized words – or 'thinking chunks' – that Dr de Bono defines here in terms of their usage to help the reader use them as tools of expression.

BY THE SAME AUTHOR

The Use of Lateral Thinking

This book is a textbook of creativity. It shows how the habit of lateral thinking can be encouraged, how new ideas can be generated. Edward de Bono has worked out special techniques for doing this, in groups or alone, and the result is a triumph of entertaining education.

Practical Thinking

How is it that in an argument both sides are always right? How is it that no one ever makes a mistake on purpose but that mistakes get made? These are some of the questions that Edward de Bono answers in this book. His theme is everyday thinking, how the mind actually works – not how philosophers think it should work.

The Mechanism of Mind

In this fascinating and provocative book Dr de Bono illustrates with simple analogies the mind's tendency to create and consolidate rigid patterns, to build myths, to polarize and divide, and then relates these mechanisms to the various modes of thinking – natural, logical, mathematical and lateral.

The Five-Day Course in Thinking

This book offers a series of simple but intriguing problems in thinking that require no special knowledge and no mathematics. The problems are designed to let the reader find out about his own personal style of thinking, its weaknesses and strengths, and the methods, latent in himself, that he never uses. Being right is not always important – an error can often lead to the right decision.

also published

Po: Beyond Yes and No
Lateral Thinking for Management
Conflicts: A Better Way to Resolve Them
Children Solve Problems
Atlas of Management Thinking

Future Positive
Opportunities
Six Thinking Hats
Lateral Thinking